IN BROAD DAYLIGHT

IN BROAD DAYLIGHT

Movies and Spectators after the Cinema

GABRIELE PEDULLÀ

Translated by Patricia Gaborik

VERSO

London • New York

This English-language edition first published by Verso 2012
© Verso 2012
Translation © Patricia Gaborik 2012
First published as *In piena luce. I nuovi spettatori e il sistema delle arti*
© Bompiani 2008

1 3 5 7 9 10 8 6 4 2

Verso
UK: 6 Meard Street, London W1F 0EG
US: 20 Jay Street, Suite 1010, Brooklyn, NY 11201
www.versobooks.com

Verso is the imprint of New Left Books

ISBN-13: 978-1-84467-853-2

British Library Cataloguing in Publication Data
A catalogue record for this book is available from the British Library

Library of Congress Cataloging-in-Publication Data

Pedullà, Gabriele.
[In piena luce. English]
In broad daylight : movies and spectators after the cinema / Gabriele Pedullà ;
translated by Patricia Gaborik.
    p. cm.
Includes bibliographical references.
ISBN 978-1-84467-853-2
1. Motion picture audiences--History. 2. Motion picture theaters--History. I. Title.
PN1995.9.A8P4813 2012
302.23'43--dc23

Typeset in Fournier by Hewer UK Ltd, Edinburgh
Printed in the US by Maple Vail

Tommaso Russo Cardona
in memoriam

Contents

Some may have loved the movie theatre more than the movie and were right to cry betrayal or suffer nostalgia. But others—myself included— preferred the film to the movie theatre. While the first probably loved the Saturday night ritual, the second preferred to invent a whole new series of personal liturgies in the anonymous darkness of a never-ending show. While the first were bound to the theatre and its rituals, the second already had a foot in the flow of the moving images. While the first would never be able to console themselves over their lost object—let's say Casablanca *or* Les enfants du paradis—*the second were ready to follow theirs to the ends of the earth and even far from the earth, all the way to the television.*

Serge Daney, *Le salaire du ʒappeur*

One mustn't regret.

René Barjavel, *Cinéma total*

Introduction

One might think that the evolution of the cinema is an artistic evolution, that cinema evolves because artists demand change. Instead I believe that such evolution is dictated by the progress of technology. Technology, the sensitivity of film, provokes changes that are much more important than artistic volition.

Andrzej Wajda

Like the world, and like cinema itself in the course of the last century, the spectator has changed.

Jean-Louis Comolli, "Suspension du spectacle"

The age of cinema, it is commonly claimed, is now drawing to a close. Day after day signs of a profound change in our relationship with moving images proliferate. The winnowing of box office receipts, the shrinking size of the audience, the decreasing time lag between a film's theatrical release and its commercialization on video, television's growing cultural prestige: these indications—at once social, economic, and aesthetic—only make the prophecy all the more credible. If cinema for decades represented the standard and even optimal filmic experience, the touchstone for all other forms of viewing, this formerly undisputed and indisputable centrality is today contested at its very core.

Perhaps, quite simply, a center no longer exists. In recent years the success of new means of image-reproduction has rendered the equation of cinema (the art of the film) with cinema (the place where films are shown) ever more fallacious. This ambiguity emerges with greater ease in languages such as Italian, French, Spanish, Portuguese, and German, which do not distinguish between the two through the use of different terms, as American English does by referring to the place as the *movie theatre* or *picture house*. Bit by bit, we have become indifferent to whether we see a film on widescreen with Dolby Surround, on an eighteen- or forty-two-inch TV, on a laptop, or on our mobile phones. And the new generation will not even feel deprived for never having seen the work of their beloved directors and divas on the big screen.

The transformation of technology and viewing habits has rendered instantly obsolete the questions that engaged intellectuals and cinephiles for decades. Who really wonders any longer whether the movie on TV last night was exactly the same as it was two years ago at the Rex or the Flora? The movie theatre's decline and cinematic memory's defection from film to video have forever delegitimized queries of that sort. From a technical point of view, the differences are not negligible, but they are not absolute either. It is true, for instance, that on television, films run at a rate of twenty-six frames per second in Europe and thirty in the United States instead of the filmic twenty-four, and thus are slightly shortened; it is also true that the small screen's format reframes the images, sacrificing their edges. But the list of grievances could go on. The TV image is much less defined, and only thanks to the small screen size does it not appear unpleasantly grainy: in the American standard, video has a total of approximately 350,000 pixels per frame, whereas a 35mm negative instead has the equivalent of about 7 million pixels—a net ratio of 1:20. The same goes for color. While television is capable of producing a maximum contrast (the relationship between the image's darkest and lightest parts) of 30:1, film can obtain a contrast factor of 120:1—four times as high. As a result, when a film is transferred to video, its colors become more luminous and intense, and the density and gradations of its blacks are immediately lost. The subtlest shadings consequently disappear.

As Francesco Savio, one of the masters of Italian film criticism, wrote, "their dynamic qualities and tonal contrasts impoverished, movies on video are like gauze dipped in milk, whereas, projected, they reach the screen uncorrupted, on the straight and flexible rays of their own light." It would be easy to compile an anthology of protests against the degradation films suffer on the small screen; such a volume would unite a large number of the last century's great directors, from John Ford ("Your name is on it, but it isn't the thing you did") to David Cronenberg ("The versions of *The Dead Zone* and *The Fly* that you find on video carry my name, and they are the films that I made, but I hate the way they look on tape. Too bright"). Generations of cinephiles—those who always specify that, alas, they saw this or that film *only* on TV—have insisted on a radical difference between the two media. But today such attitudes seem, at the very least, outmoded. The technological gap no longer seems reason enough to divide into pieces a world of moving images that is already perceived as a whole in everyday life. The purism of the big screen's champions and their almost religious cult of the movie theatre seem to have been vanquished by the common sense of the man on the street, who has never wondered whether *La Dolce Vita* on TV might be truly, deeply different from *La Dolce Vita* at the movies. Or perhaps it is the victory of the empiricism of Hollywood's tycoons, who from the start essentially saw the upstart box as a tool for recycling and converting older films—potentially the vastest distribution system of all time—and were only divided on the strategies of commercial exploitation. That it was these same people who tried to counteract the fall in ticket sales by adding something new to the big screen (color, panoramic format, 3-D, and stereo sound), as if they were reiterating the superiority of the movie theatre, is maybe the best confirmation that the average spectator was already little inclined to distinguish between the two viewing experiences.

Today the ritual of moviegoing still exists, but it represents just one of countless varieties of image-consumption; in fact, the possibility of comparing these variations allows us better to appreciate the superior technical quality of a modern multiplex. While directors of the old guard, like Chris Marker ("On television, you can see the shadow of a film, the trace of a film, the nostalgia, the echo of a film, but never the film") or Jean Eustache ("You can discover a film only at the movie theatre") were certain that there was a precise hierarchy, since the days of their youth there has been a decisive metamorphosis in the public's attitude toward films. Given their constant multiplication, the means of image-reproduction have never been so unimportant, and even the movie theatre's prestige among moving-image systems seems destined for the list of twentieth-century fetishes we are preparing to bid farewell to once and for all. It is only a matter a time.

The seeds of this situation were sown long ago—very long ago if we measure the last forty years against the rather brief history of moving images, from Edison and Lumière onward. As an irreversible phenomenon, the picture house crisis dates back at least to the blight of the 1960s and '70s, when in about a decade—both in Europe and the United States—most of the neighborhood locales that assured the dissemination of movies throughout smaller urban centers forever closed their doors. In a single blow, an entire world seemed to vanish into nothing. More directors have told this story than anyone, even if not a few novelists or critics have brought to life the experience of a long militancy of "film eaters," as Italian critic and screenwriter Enzo Ungari called them. The never-ending discoveries of the movie theatre, its erotic energy, its unconventional (and thus all the more fascinating) audiences, the attraction/repulsion of the darkness . . . and yet, despite the wonderful pages of writers like Italo Calvino, Jean-Paul Sartre, and Leonardo Sciascia, or of critics like Serge Daney and Ungari, it is above all directors who have taken inspiration from this decisive transformation. It is certainly no coincidence that, in just a few years, many very different cineastes (but with a striking predominance of Italians) felt the need to pay a melancholy-tinged homage to the cinema of their youth. From Peter Bogdanovich to Federico Fellini, from Giuseppe Tornatore to Ettore Scola, from Joe Dante to Marco Ferreri, the nostalgic evocation of the kaleidoscopic world that revolved around the picture house, with its incredible characters and their picaresque adventures, has become a subgenre of art-house films. Cinema was on the verge of leaving us, but its devotees could still celebrate, one last time, its past grandeur.

Today these films seem still too closely tied to the world of the movie house for their creators to have fully realized what this loss would eventually mean. To be fair, this is not even really what interested them. Their gaze was uniquely turned toward the past: the regret, the elegy of the good old days, and the mourning understandably got the better of the rest. The acute sense of debasement, dramatic as it was, disguised the outcome of the metamorphoses underway even when some of these directors felt the need to interrogate seriously the significance and the future repercussions of the entire process.

The intensification of the crisis and the thirty or twenty or ten years since play in our favor. Now that TV has been joined by new and stronger competitors, and cinema's marginalization within a big family of moving images seems complete, it is simply impossible to defer the question any longer. Or rather, the question has come into focus on its own—as if now, in the face of the ineluctable eclipse of the movie theatre, the stakes have suddenly become clearer.

Before the picture house had serious rivals, when going there was the only "correct" way to view a film, it was impossible to ask what role it played in the reception of movies—to ask, for example, what it meant for people during the twentieth century to attend a show sitting properly in the dark among strangers, and how such a practice influenced cinematic style. For quite some time the movie camera and the projector attracted all of the attention, leaving the theatre itself to fade into the background as less significant than those devices (which critics conventionally call the "apparatus"). The reflections of a small number of architects excepted, the movie theatre has remained the great lacuna in twentieth-century film theory.

Things changed as soon as technological innovations began to offer a wide range of possibilities and moving images were liberated from the picture house's constraints. Precisely because it has been openly challenged, the movie theatre suddenly appears right before our eyes. Only now that the frame has shed its false naturalness, thanks to the competition of new media, are we able to see it as an artificial construction that was perfected over the course of decades. It is perhaps the first time that we can fix our gaze on the movie theatre as a key institution of twentieth-century art.

Let me be clear on one point. To speak today of the picture house and its golden age, essentially from the 1920s to the 1970s, is not simply to engage in a sterile historiographical exercise. Without the movie house—without its architecture, its symbols, its behavioral codes, its rituals—the history of the seventh art would not be the one we know. But this means above all that, following the auditorium's decline, the style of films will change as well, and with it possibly the type of pleasure and aesthetic experience sought from moving images. Divested of the big screen, cinema of the future will inevitably be different from what we have had until now. As will its spectators.

In such situations, as ever, new opportunities arise and old truths are called into question. This is already happening. But, precisely because the signals coming from television and video are so contradictory, getting a clear focus on the frame—i.e. the preconditions of any given work—will help us to orient ourselves in a Janus-faced present where the old and new coexist. Anamnesis, diagnosis, and prognosis for once seem perfectly intertwined. The presence (of yesterday) and the absence (of tomorrow) can no longer be disentangled; so the gaze of the archeologist, who seeks to bring a lost experience back to life, meets that of the soothsayer, who gathers the clues of a still-undetermined future. In our historical position, any question about the movie theatre instantly involves a parallel query about its disappearance, and about a system of the arts in which the big screen has permanently abdicated its time-honored centrality. When we stop going to the movies—or go feeling as if we are doing something exceptional, as when we get decked out for the opera—films will no longer be the same. And now just one thing is certain: seen from the past (from the movie theatre's golden age, which we have already left behind), the future suddenly looks closer.

1

The Cave and the Mirror

To die, to sleep—to sleep, perchance to dream.
William Shakespeare, *Hamlet*

Everybody says, "You go to the movies to dream." That's a load of crap.
In the outskirts, you went to the movies to go to the movies.
Marco Ferreri

In the twentieth century, the auditorium was the true blind spot of film theory. Omnipresent, it remained invisible and unknowable. And yet this blindness coincided only in part with silence about the movie theatre as architectural device. Some critics did ask the question, but then—convinced it had been answered once and for all—hurried on to issues that must have seemed more necessary and urgent: photogenic quality, cinematic language, the relationship of images to physical reality, the power of editing, films' place in mass culture, the artistic charter of the new discipline . . . The paths they took to incorporate the movie theatre swiftly into reflections on the cinematic apparatus are quite interesting, though; like silences, shortcuts can be instructive—especially in a case like this, where we see a substantial unanimity of vision. It is noteworthy that, here, the main intellectual instrument used to displace the question was the analogy. Instead of beginning with the spectators' tangible conditions during the film and the way these conditions influence aesthetic reactions, as early as the 1910s film enthusiasts began to ask what a spectator resembled—as if the picture house's functioning could only be understood through a comparison.

Of the key analogies proposed—essentially two—the first and most famous is that of the cave. In the seventh book of the *Republic*, Plato had compared the philosopher to a man chained since birth in an underground den. Long convinced that movements projected on the walls of the cavern were the only form of reality, and then having escaped, this man, the story goes, turned back in order to convince his ancient prison companions of the wonders that awaited them outside of the cave, but he received in return only scorn and derision. There are, in fact, some impressive similarities between the cinema experience and Plato's story, and it is easy to see how the myth immediately became popular among early-twentieth-century film enthusiasts in a society where Latin and Greek classics still constituted a universal cultural reference. The prisoners chained to their seats, the dark, the light at their backs, the silhouettes reproducing the shapes of objects, the wall of the cave where the moving shadows are imprinted; the perfect illusion . . . How to resist the analogy's charm? How could the idea of men duped, and satisfied, by the pseudo-reality of appearances not remind us of a movie audience (despite the potentially anti-cinematic moral implicit in the Platonic condemnation of any fiction as a copy of a copy, and therefore simply a lie)?

Some probably perceived the risk in presenting spectators as prisoners of a nonexistent world, but the possibility of following Plato must have been too enticing to refuse. In search of a cultural ennobling for cinema, the contributors to film journals of the 1910s and '20s (the very first to have proposed the image of the cave as an interpretive model for the picture house) had good reason to hope that the classical allusion would offer the newcomer the quarterings of nobility required for admission into the empyrean of the respectable arts. Since then, the danger of providing cinema's detractors with an argument against it seems to have been of no great concern. On the contrary, the lengthy list of those who, if only in passing, drew on the image of the cave (Edgar Morin, Jean-Louis Baudry, Christian Metz, Vilém Flusser . . .) best confirms the difficulty of doing without the illustrious antecedent. Even Jacques Derrida, in an interview with *Cahiers du cinéma* in 2001, could not avoid using the same parallel.

Once it was established that the movie theatre reproduced the Platonic cave and that films were able to captivate and deceive spectators with a force of persuasion unknown by any other art, it did not seem necessary to further interrogate the nature, the powers, and the functions of this marvelous engine. All we needed to know about the auditorium was that Plato had in some ways "foreseen" it, not unlike how Leonardo da Vinci had "invented" the tank or the helicopter. In the name of Socrates, Cratylus, and Phaedo, any question could be laid to rest.

It is maybe in part for this reason that the second analogy appeared much later; in its mature form it dates back just to the 1970s, when for the first time—facing the crisis of the traditional circuits—spectators, critics, and directors began to realize that one of the fundamental pieces of the filmic experience as they had known it was disappearing. At the heart of the new theory was the conviction (psychoanalytic in origin, but having taken root enough in common parlance) that this experience is fundamentally like dreaming though we are awake—a condition similar to hypnosis. From here the logic was simple. If going to the movies is equivalent to dreaming, and if indeed there exists a specific relationship between the effects induced by film and by hypnosis (enrapture, the breaking down of barriers, projecting oneself into the picture), the movie theatre cannot help but encourage the spectator's total relaxation: make him receptive to being kidnapped by the flow of images. The dark, the silence, and the comfortable seats would be all the elements needed to conquer the last resistance of those present, putting them in a state of passivity quite similar to that of a person who sleeps. Exactly as a hypnotic (or psychoanalytical) session has its rituals incorporating metallic pendulums, leather sofas, and commands, to work correctly cinema would also need a precise ceremonial; the auditorium with its darkness, its silence, and its immobility would play a part. The movie palace as gigantic psychoanalytical sofa.

Though the cave analogy remained at a purely intuitive level, its implications never fully developed except by those who used it to revile cinema's deception outright, the analogy with the dream and hypnosis has a richer history. Less "cultured" (one need not have read Plato, or even Freud, to understand its premises), in the end it offered the only real attempt to explain "scientifically" how viewing conditions influence the spectator during the projection of a film. The credit goes to French critic and novelist Jean-Louis Baudry, who, examining the relationship between dream activity and the cinematic experience, proposed an elaborate theoretical model at the beginning of the 1970s. According to Baudry, who took as his points of departure Lacan's psychoanalysis and Althusser's Marxism, cinema's allure—before that of any single film—lies in the resemblance between the position of the spectator and the mental condition of the infant during the so-called "mirror phase," when the child produces a first sketch of the idea of "I" while observing his or her own reflection. The physical immaturity of the motor apparatus and the precocious development of the infant's vision correspond exactly to the experience of the public watching a film. Both are characterized by the dark, the absence of movement, the predominance of viewing over any other activity, the impression that the images are real, and the impossibility of verifying this reality—not to mention the fact that some psychoanalysts describe dreams as images projected on a screen, just as in a film. The desire to relive one's own infancy with an illusory sense of control over moving pictures would thus be sufficient to explain the twentieth century's burning passion for the new art. For Baudry, in fact, cinema's appeal lay entirely in its capacity to transform any audience member into a "transcendental subject," virtually placed at the center of the universe. From this would stem the medium's ideological nature—idealizing and potentially conservative—but also its strength and its necessity, if one must read the Platonic myth as a psychic projection of a primitive desire inscribed in the minds of man since the beginning of time.

Baudry's proposal, taken up by Roland Barthes and Christian Metz, is still quite popular, especially among scholars who include psychoanalysis (not necessarily Lacanian) in their arsenals. Problem solved, then? Absolutely not. Despite the undeniable kinship, there are plenty of reasons to think that neither the cave nor the dream parallel adequately explains what happens in the movie theatre. The problem, of course, is not in the use of analogy; authoritative philosophers have shown that even logic sometimes works through analogic reasoning. However, comparisons can be good or bad, indispensable or completely misleading. Everything depends on their ability to show the similarities of essential elements without being led astray by superficial affinities. And as soon as we look less hastily, the two analogies reveal themselves to be deceitful, that is, built upon dubious consonances.

The American cognitive film theorists—and in particular Noël Carroll—have shown the argumentative fallacies behind the image of the movie theatre as a modern Platonic cave. Unlike the *Republic*'s prisoners, spectators can always get up and leave, or move their heads; the projected image does not always come from behind the spectators (there is such thing as rear-projection); nothing requires us to read the Platonic myth as the manifestation of an atavistic desire to return to infancy; and so forth. Just as facile, then, is the comparison of a film to dream or hypnosis that is so fundamental to Baudry's thesis. In this case the list of objections is impressive: even if it is less comfortable, the cinematic apparatus works just as well with spectators who are not seated; movies are not solipsistic like dreams, because anyone can discuss his response with the person next to him; the public is always aware it is in a dark room (an awareness we lose while we sleep); frames are detailed, whereas dream images are often partial and incomplete . . .

Here, too, the list could go on. Yet for our discussion the decisive point is a different one: the extreme confusion about why the movie theatre was made and why people love to see films. The analogies with the cave and the mirror become objectionable first of all because they obscure the particular nature—artistic, or even just recreational—of the cinematic experience. French symbolist Rémy de Gourmont put it well back in 1907, when the idea of the equivalence of film and dream began to spread among the first timid admirers of the new art (Sigmund Freud's book on the interpretation of dreams, not by chance, had come out in 1900): "The public doesn't go to the cinema to dream; they go to enjoy themselves." It would be hard to find a more perfect formula to clear away the relics of the analogies with the cave and the mirror phase. The argument that the pleasure of going to the movies really depends on a desire to regress to infancy lacks validity, too, because in this case it would be necessary to explain how it is therefore possible that people watch films with the same satisfaction on television or on their laptop:

that is to say, in radically different conditions than those which Baudry judges essential for the full unfolding of the seductive power of moving images.

What we risk losing with such interpretations is first and foremost the *aesthetic function* for which the movie house was imagined. When this banal observation—that people go freely to the theatre to take pleasure from moving pictures—is accounted for, the spectator's resemblance to Plato's prisoner or Lacan's infant becomes irrelevant. Let us begin with Plato. How do we ignore the fact that at the movies spectators *are not* deceived, but rather buy a ticket to attend a show and have a story told to them, just as when they read a novel or go to the playhouse? That we appreciate films *not* as an alternative to life but as a pause, an intermission, a parenthesis in our daily activities, while Plato's men are spellbound from the start in a copy of the world which for them constitutes the only reality ("from their childhood," as specified in the *Republic*)? That Samuel Taylor Coleridge's "willing suspension of disbelief," implicit in every fiction, presupposes a kind of illusion completely different from that experienced by Plato's men, prisoners of shadows and therefore incapable of seeing the only things that truly exist—namely, ideas?

Not every viewing experience is the same viewing experience, just as not every deception is the same deception—especially if we participate knowingly and willingly. When we consider this simple point, very little remains of the similarities that at the beginning seemed so significant. This is all the truer because the comparison with Plato's cave seems designed to justify a rejection of cinema for being an instrument of ideological falsification and oppression: an argument against the new medium that was made often throughout the twentieth century, from the right and from the left, by such authoritative figures as Theodor W. Adorno and Georges Duhamel.

The original sin resides in this confusion, and the same could be said of the dream analogy. Cinema is not a machine for taking people back to their childhood through hypnosis, or at least no more than it is a process for distancing them from the direct contemplation of ideas. Just like Lacan's children, Plato's prisoners see something, but they do not attend a show in the same way a paying spectator does. And precisely because the Greek philosopher's preoccupations remain strictly ontological and gnoseological (What is really real? How can I recognize it?), whereas the French psychoanalyst is interested in the process leading the child to acquire the first elements of an adult consciousness (How is the subject born?), every attempt to explain cinema through an analogy with the cave or with the mirror phase enacts an undue slippage. So, we need a new strategy, as we will begin to understand the movie theatre's function only if we study it as an integral part of the cinematic apparatus: a special device, the equal of the camera or the projector, conceived for giving the spectator a kind of experience different from all others.

Compared to the Platonic myth and the child's discovery of the subject, the real workings of a movie house in action undoubtedly look less exciting. A few elements suffice: a room, not necessarily big; a white wall or a big screen to project images onto; a series of seats or armchairs (though in old-time theatres people sat on the floor or stood if there were no places left); an opening opposite the screen for light to pass through. Such simple furnishings discouraged additional investigation. And yet, in its minimalism, this structure is the result of a long process of definition led by tradespeople and architects so that the film could work, if not in the best way (as we shall see, in fact, there was not just one), at least in the way that they thought best served their interests—that is to say, to maximize the spectators' reactions and, in so doing, sell more seats.

The apparent simplicity of the solutions adopted for the movie house might remind us of another twentieth-century aesthetic device: the art gallery. In this case, comparison can be useful. As Brian O'Doherty has recounted, this too is a locale that seems neutral, but whose every detail has been studied in advance so as to obtain the desired effect: to favor the appreciation of the works by a viewer who is always also a potential buyer. So that this can happen—so that the art can "take on its own life"—a gallery must meet a series of extremely precise requirements or risk rapid failure. The size and shape of the spaces, color, lighting, furniture, acoustics: nothing can be left to chance. The fact that the code remains implicit does not mean that its prescriptions—its *musts* and *must nots*—are not managed extremely rigorously; on the contrary, as always, the most constricting laws are those of which we are not even aware.

Unlike film historians, though, art historians began long ago to inter-rogate the conventions of the gallery device, and now we can devise a sort of elementary pentalogy for the aspiring gallery manager, from the shaded windows (to keep the outside world out) and the ceiling lights as the only illumination, to the uniform white of the walls and the parquet flooring or soft moquette (evidently to lend a sense of luxury and comfort that puts the visitor at ease, preparing her for the encounter with beauty), all the way to the imperative of keeping the spaces completely empty, except for the works of art, properly separated so that each can "breathe" (a modest desk at the entrance being the only piece of furniture allowed).

As common and insignificant as they might seem, each of these elements makes its own contribution, at once real and symbolic, to the institution that connoisseurs call simply "the white cube." This is the official residence of Art: a room without shadows, white, clean, and artificial—ascetic as a clinic and cold as a cenotaph to the unknown soldier. Comfortable but also a tad inhospitable (just enough to make visitors maintain the required respectful attitude), purposely conceived so that the works of art can display themselves in a sort of defensive eternity, removed from time and its vagaries.

From the moment they cross the threshold, visitors must clearly perceive that they have entered a separate space. In the end it is precisely this separation that guarantees the gallery's efficacy, almost as if the closed space has the power to transform the most banal object into a work of art simply because it is on display there. An aesthetic response will inevitably follow an aesthetic question: this is the first and perhaps principal lesson of Marcel Duchamp's ready-mades. Urinals, torn post-ers, shit in a box: anything can be worthy of appreciation when placed in the right context, given that the gallery itself is "art-in-potency" in its purest state.

All of this, naturally, has its price. The gallery not only encourages the aesthetic participation of its visitors, but also, in an anxiety of purity, proclaims its own distance from the outside world, imposing pre-emptive sanctions on any attempt to break down boundaries. Protected from the effects of contact with everyday life, which goes on undisturbed, the white cube resembles a limbo where, while the eyes and the mind are always welcome, the body is barely tolerated, giving rise to a curious Cartesian paradox in which the visitor is and is not there at the same time, entirely absorbed in the contemplation of the work—the only legitimate activity in a space dedicated to this single end.

But the picture house? At first glance, it seems a world away from the white cube. Child of the Boulevard theatre, with its chaotic and noisy public, cinema is the mass art-form of the twentieth century; partly for this reason, the separation of the auditorium from the world outside had been incomplete. No hushed atmosphere, no select clientele, no promise of social climbing. Regular moviegoers had nothing to do with this culture of distinction. Instead there were the couples making out in the dark; the adolescents who skipped school for a matinee and commented on every single scene; the immigrants who needed someone to translate the silent film placards written in a language they did not yet understand and perhaps never would; the workers who took advantage of the venue's bathroom for their Sunday *toilette* . . . This is the world that directors have nostalgically depicted since the 1970s: boisterous, lively, multifaceted, even suspect and illegal, but for all of these reasons also absolutely irresistible. Comprehensibly, this intense social life centering on the picture house has conditioned and continues to condition our idea of twentieth-century cinema. In historians' accounts, the public always appears invested in every activity but paying attention to what is on screen. Instead of watching the audience during the decisive moment—while it views the film—for the most part we see it daydreaming just before the projection begins, or remembering the movie when the show is all over, and often not even that: as soon as the screen lights up, the scholar's eye turns elsewhere, wanders through the aisles, infiltrates the administrative offices, or escapes to the foyer, in search of new adventures.

Here remains a gap to be filled. Fascinated by moviegoing as an occasion for meeting and socializing, historians have looked at the auditorium as a place where one does everything but watch a film; a place saturated with lives and passions, and precisely for this reason so intriguing; a little microcosm where, almost by chance and as an accessory activity, someone projects a movie. It is not difficult to see why this happened. Focusing on empirical audiences was a way to dismantle the abstractions of Baudry's, Barthes's, and Metz's psychoanalytic models and give space to the plurality of experience that theory seemed to want to erase with a single stroke of its pen; differences existed, and it was necessary to deal with them even at the cost of an abrupt shift toward the social history that would once again obscure the aesthetic problematic. But are we sure that we still ought to talk today of the movie house in the same essentially legendary terms as do *Amarcord* and *The Last Picture Show*? The end of the movie theatre epoch and the beginning of a new spectatorial regime make a rethinking of such convictions urgent. If the human heat surrounding that which we might call "the dark cube" or "the opaque cube" (according to a poetic definition by Barthes) has completely monopolized the critics' attention, generating the equivocation by which the house is studied more as the intersection of histories than as an aesthetic technology or meaning-making machine, it is time to correct this distorted vision, or at least supplement it with a new perspective. We need a Copernican revolution that will refocus the terms of the debate.

In the twentieth century the movie theatre was not a chaotic place of socialization, but a steely modernist device—or rather, it was not one more than the other (even if, as we will see, its origins date back at least four centuries). No less than the art gallery, the auditorium represented an "other" space, carefully distinguished from the world in which we live our normal lives. And just as the white walls and the lights eventually began to seem important to art historians, from now on the auditorium will have to be studied first and foremost as an *aesthetic technology* designed to encourage the spectator's concentration.

No one, perhaps, has affirmed the conventional nature of the movie theatre's protocol as clearly as Peter Greenaway:

> Cinema is like an elaborate game with rules. The aim of the game is to successfully suspend disbelief. The audience has been well trained over some eighty years of practice. Necessary circumstances are darkness and a bright projection bulb and a screen. The audience agree to enter a dark space and sit facing in one direction. They will be prepared to sit for some two hours—usually in the evenings.

Greenaway's comment could be further developed, highlighting, for example, the spectator's increased willingness to remain immobile in the dark on the weekend, or the often decisive function that the evening show has occupied in the first dates of new couples (cinema as aphrodisiac of the masses?). But what really counts here is the estrangement of the gaze that enables us to observe the cinematic liturgy as something not at all obvious—a social practice that today seems self-evident only because we have been habituated to it since infancy, in this respect truly similar to the experience of Plato's prisoners. Culture disguised as nature: exactly like the art gallery of immaculate walls and sparkling parquet.

The timelines are not even very far apart. Just like the movie theatre, the gallery, at least in its current form, is a fairly recent institution, more or less the child of impressionism. Only at the end of the nineteenth century did the austere and somewhat aristocratic space we know today emerge, definitively wiping out the eighteenth-century picture galleries with their tendency to amass paintings of very different sizes, periods, artists, subjects, and qualities alongside one other. It is not so strange, then, that the golden age of the "white cube" coincided with the most glorious season of the "dark cube": from the 1920s until the 1970s, when artists increasingly profaned the gallery's codes and confines, as everyone began to perceive the entirely conventional nature of the setting. From Yves Klein to Joseph Kosuth, from Christo and Jeanne-Claude to Maurizio Cattelan, a whole current of contemporary art has worked to demystify the exhibition space and its sacred aura.

The coincidence is not without import. Indeed, just as today some propose that we see in the gallery the greatest realization of artistic modernism, we can ask if something similar should not be said with regard to the movie theatre—if, in other words, in the eyes of future generations, it will not be the seats in parallel rows and the oversized screen that were the true core of twentieth-century cinema, far more than directors' styles, generic conventions, or national schools. Obviously, aesthetic devices like the gallery and the auditorium do not change the works of art they host, but they can influence, even quite profoundly, the visitors' or viewers' reactions to them; they impose, in other words, a precise style of *viewing* and of *listening*. Reformulated in these terms, even the question of the relationship that exists between *La Dolce Vita* projected in large format and its video versions viewed at home acquires new interest. While we cannot talk about difference in the terms we do for a print with respect to its original painting, for two editions of the same book, or for two performances of the same song, any notion of perfect identicalness is likewise inapplicable.

The response will always inevitably be twofold: yes, the film on TV is substantially the same as the one we see at the theatre; no, the experience of the film is not identical because different aesthetic devices differently condition our attitude toward the work. As a result, the small screen cannot be treated as simply a downgraded dark cube, almost as if it were merely a question of degree—of better or worse—with respect to an ever-unattainable ideal of the image's absolute presence.

The need to study the conditions in which a work of art is presented to its public does not obviously only regard moving images. There is an unbridgeable distance between a Francesco Petrarch sonnet read quietly in private and the same sonnet sounded in a theatre by a great actor's voice, even when not a comma has been altered (never mind the possibility that it might be sung to a Claudio Monteverdi tune); but the same could be said for a play (silent reading, staged reading, dress rehearsal, full production . . .) or for a piece of music, as dancing a waltz by Strauss involves a participation and a pleasure very different from listening to it while relaxing in an armchair. The words of the play text or the notes of a piece of music remain the same, but it would be hard to speak of an identical experience. As Walter Benjamin once wrote, discussing a similar problem, "the power of a text is different when it is read from when it is copied out . . . because the reader follows the movement of his mind in the free flight of daydreaming, whereas the copier submits it to command."

However, it is with moving images that such an approach proves particularly fruitful, due to the contrast between the fixity of an infinitely reproducible work and the multiplicity of responses to it (which are connected to its presentation). To speak of viewing and listening styles thus means forgetting the sterile contraposition of good sense—which says that a film on the small screen should not be fundamentally different from the same film seen at the theatre—with the certainty, not just of the most demanding cinephiles, that between the two experiences an irreducible distance nonetheless remains.

This is not the only reason that today we need a unitary history of distinct aesthetic devices, from the playhouse and the picture palace to television and individual media. The concept of viewing style—fundamental to this unitary history—also helps explain why the effects of the movie theatre's crisis appeared so belatedly. The canonical date of the landing of films in American homes is usually set at 1956, when the Hollywood majors closed the first important contract with the national networks ceding broadcast rights for black-and-white films produced before 1948. It could have been a revolution; instead, from that moment on the spilling over of the most successful films from the big to the small screen produced no decisive change in the audience's behavior. For a generation or two, the theatre remained the only "normal" way to see a movie. Those who stayed at home tried to re-create the viewing conditions a picture house would have guaranteed. Lights were turned out; armchairs were placed at the right distance; someone unplugged the telephone so as not to be interrupted—during what represented a still rather exceptional event, given the limited number of showings and broadcast hours of the early years. We will have a chance to return to this problem, but what is important here is that the cinematic viewing model was so strong as to be exported even in the absence of some of the elements most characteristic of the movie theatre.

Today this relationship has been turned on its head. At just over a century since the construction of the first buildings designed to host the Lumière brothers' invention, what seems to have entered into crisis once and for all is the particular viewing style encouraged by the auditorium but so prestigious and pervasive as to be adopted elsewhere, when spectators have to resign themselves and attend a film without all of the comforts of a panoramic screen or a perfectly darkened room. If in the 1950s and '60s (but later, too) men and women watching a movie continued to behave as if they were at a picture house, regardless of the viewing conditions, today the opposite seems to be true: the movie theatre is the anomaly—the infraction of a norm and an aesthetic practice that find their codification in the domestic space.

But let us avoid any misunderstandings. To say that the age of the movie theatre is coming to an end is much different from prophesying its complete disappearance—an event that seems neither imminent nor even probable. Simply put, while the auditorium incarnated the optimal filmic experience, since at least the 1970s the monopoly of the cinematic viewing style has entered, little by little, into crisis. The picture house was first surrounded by television and then by multiple supports in competition among themselves, to such an extent that none of them can hope for the exclusivity that the movie theatres once had. In light of this phenomenon, the fact that for some years the number of venues and the volume of box office takings (but not the number of spectators) has started to grow again in the Western world is in the end an irrelevant detail. It took a few post-cinematic generations for television to escape once and for all from the tutelage of its older brother—cinema. Only in the final quarter of the last century did the new arrival enter maturity and truly begin to assert its autonomy. Actually, the process is ongoing, but the signals of an acceleration multiply, and with the fall of the movie theatre as a viewing paradigm, soon nothing will be as it was before.

The auditorium's slow decline brings with it the irreversible decay of one model of spectatorship; and, in a chain reaction, the disappearance of this spectator—which we might call "classical"—produces a radically selective memory of bygone cinema. We have all had the painful experience of discovering those films revered in our memories that on the small screen just do not "cut it." Since all of the reinforcements concocted for movies disappear at home, we are no longer surprised that so few films really hold up to the video test; and yet, with the exception of Serge Daney, few critics have explored the effects of cinema's forced domestication. On video, dark photography becomes indecipherable; crowd scenes lose any epic power; the spatial composition of panoramic formats like cinemascope is completely distorted. Never mind the stylistic choices whose meanings change when they pass from the big to the small screen, like the close-up, which today—after all the abuses of the shot/reverse shot on television—is difficult to still define as the "soul of cinema," as Jean Epstein did in the 1920s: a sort of explosion in the continuity of a film, a wrinkling of the story, where the camera's approach to objects was never gratuitous, but indicated a discovery, an emotional climax, an epiphany. There is no doubt that in the years to come the rethinking of the canon will be determined partly by old films' differing ability to adapt to the new medium.

Twentieth-century directors conceived of their films imagining them projected under very precise conditions; those conditions having disappeared, these works will suffer from the demise of the device for which they were originally envisioned. Every art continuously creates and recreates its past; but when it comes to cinema, the big screen's crisis not only accelerates this process, but also reshapes our appreciation of each movie. We need to think of twentieth-century cinema as an animal in an ecosystem; cast out of that ecosystem, films must either adapt to the new environment, survive in little protective enclaves (cineforums and national cinematheques), or simply die out. But surely, for all of them, natural selection is already underway with a violence that is unprecedented, perhaps excluding only the passage from silent films to the talkies—when it became normal for movies to "speak," and those that did not were quickly condemned to oblivion.

Even if today only a tiny portion of moving images are consumed according to the rigorous behavioral code that characterizes the dark cube, that device was the secret engine of twentieth-century cinema. And yet, precisely because we prepare to leave that season behind, it is far more certain that, without the movie theatre as we knew it, film history would be completely different—just as the movies of the past have begun to seem different, very different, since the small screen has begun to erode the auditorium's centrality. Despite appearances, the cinematic viewing style's decline has relatively little to do with our past—nostalgia for the lost Saturday night or Sunday afternoon movie ritual, the mournful cries of cinephiles for every old theatre reopened as a gym or mall, the establishment of an enduring canon. Rather, to think about the movie theatre today is to ask very precise questions about the future of moving images. While competition from television by now seems an ancient phenomenon requiring no further analysis, the change we are witnessing is something without precedent, and relates to the spectator's comprehensive attitude toward moving pictures—wherever they are.

This story coming to a close, another immediately opens up. Because the movie theatre has such a profound impact on directors' works and styles, it would certainly be surprising if its eclipse and the consequent transition from the age of cinematography to that of individual media (the disc player, the computer, the videophone . . .) did not bring with them major repercussions. This is our present, and to reconstruct the vicissitudes of the dark cube in its first century of life means principally to investigate this epochal metamorphosis just as it is happening.

2

Toward the Dark Cube

And now let us talk about places of performance.
Leon Battista Alberti, *De re aedificatoria*

We don't sell movies, we sell seats.
Michael Loew

Probably no writer has described the movie theatre experience better than Julio Cortázar. The darkness and the silence, the solitude in being part of a crowd, the ecstasy in the presence of the images, the desire to jump into the screen, the impression that you are somewhere else even as you sit among your friends or a group of strangers:

> You go to the movies or the theatre and live your night without thinking about the people who have already gone through the same ceremony, choosing the place and the time, getting dressed and telephoning and row eleven or five, the darkness and the music, territory that belongs to nobody and to everybody there where everybody is a nobody, the men or women in their seats, maybe a word of apology for arriving late, a murmured comment that someone picks up or ignores, almost always silence, looks pouring onto the stage or the screen, fleeing from what's beside them, from what's on this side.

This passage from *We Love Glenda So Much* offers an excellent starting point for reflecting on the condition of the spectator during the projection of a film, not least because of the novelist's skill in sketching the dark cube experience through a catalog of such heterogeneous details. Sight, hearing, touch . . . A hypothetical list of the elements characterizing cinematic viewing would not be much more extensive than the one we find in the brilliant opening of Cortázar's story. In the end, from the spectator's point of view, there are, in fact, only six truly important features:

1) Most importantly, the strict separation of the auditorium. The projection happens in a space completely distinct from the world outside, in which the audience is isolated for the duration of the picture. There are obviously practical reasons for this barricade (achieving the darkness needed to produce clearly visible images), but just as many symbolic reasons weigh on such a choice: the public should never forget that it has crossed a threshold and entered into an "other" space requiring absolute dedication until the last words roll off the screen and the lights come back on.

2) The (almost) total darkness, all the better perceived when we allow ourselves that somewhat estranging pleasure of the matinee only to exit at the end of the film to find that it is no longer daytime. "What hit me on coming out," Italo Calvino wrote, "was the sense of time having passed, the contrast between two different temporal dimensions, inside and outside the film. I had gone in in broad daylight, and came out to find it dark, the lamp-lit streets prolonging the black-and-white of the screen." Emergency lighting apart, the dark cube banishes any light source that is not the projector; for this reason, before the massive fire-repellent doors of the modern multiplex (and the rigorous prohibition on entering once the film has started), there was a heavy double curtain that prevented latecomers from disturbing the other spectators by letting light in. "One can't evade an iris. Round about, blackness; nothing to attract one's attention," Jean Epstein commented, in a 1921 essay celebrating the auditorium's hypnotic power. But let us not forget that light and darkness become language, too: just like at the playhouse, dimming lights tell the audience the show is about to begin, and in many European countries some lights remain on during the pre-film commercials in order to

better mark their difference from the movie, which, on the contrary, is to be respectfully appreciated in complete darkness.

3–4) The spectator's immobility and silence. Notwithstanding the numerous exceptions to these two principles (especially in the cheap theatres—the historians' true delight, as we have seen), the movie house's behavioral code requires patrons to refrain from disturbing one another by moving about or talking. Failing to respect these rules would damage a venue's reputation, it is understood, and it is in the proprietor's best interest to discourage such behavior. The manuals that the Hollywood majors distributed to theatre operators in the 1930s recommended absolute inflexibility on this point: ushers needed to keep watch so that no one talked during the show; in the case of infractions, after two warnings, on the third offense violators were to be politely but firmly escorted to the exit.

5) The large screen size. Though the dimensions range widely from one auditorium to the next, filmed reality is always presented as "larger than life," even to the extent that a detail of an actor's face can cover the whole screen. (Generally speaking, screens grew in the 1950s as an effect of the diffusion of panoramic formats, shrank after the arrival of urban multiplexes, and expanded again with the appearance of the suburban multiplex, where space is not an issue.)

6) The communal (or in any case non-domestic) nature of the cinematic experience. The picture house is accessible to everyone who buys a ticket, and this means that the viewing happens among strangers, usually in seats of parallel rows, even if other formations remain possible, as in the auditoriums that have maintained the old playhouse structure's side boxes. In any case, at the movies you are in company. Like Cortázar said, it is the "territory that belongs to nobody and to everybody there where everybody is a nobody."

As distinct as they seem from one another, all six elements move toward the same goal. This quick list already enables us to see the movie theatre's particular contribution to the show: it facilitates the aesthetic response to the visual and aural entreaties coming from the screen, and protects the public from distractions. But this is the exact movie theatre that we are acquainted with; in other words, we run the risk that the dark cube's decisive role in the history of moving-image systems will be made invisible by force of habit. Moviegoers today finds themselves in a position not unlike that of the contemporary art enthusiast who takes for granted the rarified and somewhat icy atmosphere of the gallery because this is the only environment with which he associates an exhibition. The cinema experience is indissolubly connected to these six elements, to such an extent that it seems nearly impossible to distinguish them from technologies of image recording and projection (broadly speaking, even open-air and drive-in theatres follow the same model).

Yet in reality, things are much different: the place that now seems so "obvious" struggled for twenty or thirty years to establish itself and its particular viewing style worldwide, and it had to contend with a series of alternative solutions, discarded only after a long battle. So, if we truly want to understand the movie theatre's importance to cinema's first century (and thus the consequences of its current marginalization, too), we must go back to the 1910s and '20s, when the adoption of a specific model of architecture and of spectacle went together with a particular idea of the apparatus.

In this case, the marriage of history and theory can yield pleasant surprises. We have seen how the cinema we know is closely tied to separation from the outside world, to the dark, and to the spectator's silence and immobility. As Jean Epstein wrote in the early 1920s, "Wrapped in darkness, ranged in cell-like seats, directed toward the source of emotion by their softer side, the sensibilities of the entire auditorium converge as if in a tunnel, toward the film. Everything else is barred, excluded, no longer valid." And yet it was not always that way. The fundamental requisites that today's audience associate with a movie theatre became a stable fixture at the end of a long process that can be considered complete only with the universal diffusion of the sound film. To say that the golden age of cinema roughly covered the same decades in which the art gallery enjoyed an unmatched prestige—from the 1920s to the beginning of the 1970s—is to exclude at least a quarter-century, if the count begins with the Lumière brothers' first public projection on December 28, 1895 at the Café des Capucines in Paris. Just like the art gallery, it was only little by little—adjustment by adjustment and correction by correction—that a single standard was established: the white cube or the black cube, the completely empty room or the rows of seats, light from above or absolute darkness.

Before this happened, before the creation of a space expressly designed to host projections, the film experience was something quite different. Luckily, contemporary accounts give us a good idea of what it meant to see a movie for the first few decades of the last century. Still in the 1920s, when the movie theatre as we know it was just one of many hypotheses, it was not unusual for a journalist to dedicate half of his article to the merits, defects, and peculiarities of a theatre rather than to the film of the day. It is thus entertaining to discover the pioneers of film criticism as they classify the setting according to the public it served, the orchestra's energy, or the attendants' politeness; as they castigate the other customers' less than impeccable manners; or as they comment with impressive competence on the quality of the drinks, or maybe the comfort of the seats (the leather padding or the rough wooden benches), the cleanliness, and the service. Entertaining, but above all instructive, because their words give us a better idea of the conditions under which a film was projected in those very first years, when anything and everything was still possible.

It is worth quoting at least one example at length:

> The Winter Garden at Antwerp is a nice place. Should we call it a café-concert? Should we call it a movie house? When you enter, it's hard to know for sure if you're among a crowd of earnest schoolgirls or in a music hall. Both, I think. But it is lovely; the room never ends and it has six long parallel rows of tables that remind you of a wedding banquet. You drink, the music makes an infernal racket (in proportion!). Smartly uniformed ushers hurry the spectators along; it doesn't smell bad, and it's ventilated. The ticket for this paradoxical place costs twenty cents.

Thus wrote Louis Delluc (along with Jean Epstein, a future leading cineaste of the French Impressionist Cinema of the 1920s) in an article dated July 8, 1919, in the euphoria of the first months of peace after the close of the Great War. The sounds, the colors, and the odors of the Winter Garden will surprise a non-specialist reader today first and foremost because they furnish an idea of cinematic conviviality extremely distant from our own, where the film constitutes just one of the various ingredients of the entertainment—perhaps not even the most important one.

And yet the Winter Garden is hardly exceptional, as the pages of any journalist of the period—not just Delluc—would lead us to conclude. There is the Marivaux in Paris, with its British dancers and their acrobatic numbers; there is the movie house on the Avenue de la Gare, in Nice, with a bar so illuminated there does not seem light enough left for the projector; or the Majestic at Nîmes, so much like a "well-run garage"—a talented projectionist, drinking binges, the Catholics separated from the Protestants and the French from the Spanish. Or, finally, there is the auditorium on Paris's rue de la Roquette, the algid temple of the new art that sought to imitate those already in Munich, Berlin, Vienna, and Amsterdam, which more closely resemble the spaces familiar to us today.

Delluc's articles describe a situation not only French: at the beginning of the 1920s there still was no single viewing style for films, and in the large majority of cases the silence and order of our movie theatres was as yet very far off. A broad range of solutions remained open, though it is important to note that places like the one on the rue de la Roquette represented an exception. If Delluc described the picture house as an eminently *promiscuous* environment, this term should be understood first in the sense that many very different and often opposed functions were brought together in a single space: part restaurant, part bordello, part theatre, and a touch of the fair. For this reason, it is not only the Winter Garden that seems a "paradoxical place," but each and every early picture house: sanctuary of images and noisy multicolored cavea with its contrasting vocations, between heaven and hell. "It has affinities with both church and alcove," English architectural connoisseur Philip

Morton Shand would write in 1930, with a touch of irony toward the sumptuous electicism of the new movie palaces. But above all, thanks to Delluc, we realize that, before the movie theatre's triumph, seeing the film was not necessarily the main reason to go to the cinema; the pleasure of the unknown and the not always upright reputation of the men and women who frequented it must have played an important role in the effusive passion for the new art: elements that, if anything, made it even more captivating, as cinephiles of the 1910s and '20s made abundantly clear.

We get a sense of what this plebian and itinerant cinema was like if we turn Delluc's observations about the Winter Garden inside out. For each of his points of praise we can imagine the slightly disturbing reality of its opposite: nasty odors, lack of ventilation, equivocal encounters, uncomfortable seats. But more importantly, when it comes to a discussion of the auditorium as aesthetic device, what strikes us is its radically different viewing conditions from those of cinema's classical age. Of the six elements characterizing cinematic viewing style, in fact, only screen size and the collective projections (points five and six) seem guaranteed in the case of the first picture houses:

1) No separation from the outside world. On the contrary, we have an open space where people wander freely, setting their own rhythm for the evening's entertainment, moving from one area to the other, breaking up the viewing of the film with other activities. Such behavior is encouraged by the program's extreme brevity and by the alternation of live and recorded performances.

2) No absolute darkness—a condition that in places like the Winter Garden seems neither attainable nor, to tell the truth, always desirable. Even without addressing the light needed by the members of the orchestra to read their music (when there is no player piano), newspapers of the period often speak of rose-colored lights kept on during the show to avoid a complete darkness that would have keep more timid types away.

3–4) No quiet and immobility on the part of the spectators. At the Winter Garden, as in many theatres, it is perfectly normal for those who watch the show to do other things simultaneously—eat, drink, chit-chat. Most importantly, spectators do not deliver themselves to silence (rather, as we gather from Delluc, it is quite probable that music and voices fill the room), partly because they do not always sit in straight lines facing the screen, as there are small tables for holding drinks and snacks, commonly arranged in rows emanating out from the center, in a semi-circle.

As soon as we consider the conditions of cinema at the beginning of the twentieth century—a technical marvel with an at best dubious artistic stature, like the X-ray—the reasons for this anarchy are clear. Perfectly contemporaneous, the discoveries of the Lumière brothers and the Curies were often paired in theatrical posters and newspaper reports as must-see modern wonders: the life of shadows and the mystery of fluorescence alongside the bearded lady and elephant man (as David Lynch well understood, *Elephant Man* being one of his many films about cinema and its tricks). This uncertainty surely did not help to set a single standard. Still lacking a space expressly dedicated to projections, movies were forced to seek hospitality elsewhere, and it was perfectly normal that they wound up leaning on other, often older kinds of spectacle, and being conditioned by them. The "cinema," each time, was where the projector was: in a café or a temporarily empty garage, under a circus tent, at a fair, on an improvised vaudeville stage. This precarious condition recalls the medieval theatre, when, in the absence of a special building for performances, it was up to the actors to "theatricalize" the spaces of daily life through their presence, and a show could be held just about anywhere—on a street corner as in a market square, in the aisles of a church, or on a platform erected for the occasion in a palace courtyard.

Theatre's nomadic conditions before the codification of an architectural place of performance naturally involved a tremendous willingness to adjust to very diverse contexts, but we find these same effects of a wandering existence in the early cinema as well. At the beginning of the century—when the program changed according to the location and occasion in which the film was being shown—vaudeville and fairground theatres, cafés, and circuses not only gave hospitality to the projection, but also decisively influenced the audience's reaction. Condemned to maximum versatility, the early cinema had no choice but to be absorbed by a larger show and, above all, to be contaminated by less demanding forms of entertainment. In the 1920s, films would have a lot to be forgiven for, as cinema struggled to be counted among the respectable disciplines, on the same level as music or literature—so much so that avant-garde directors' insistence on the concept of "pure cinema" (an entirely cinematic cinema, completely freed of its borrowings from the sister arts) seems the natural correlate to the desire to cleanse films of contact with all that was impure.

Only the picture house's institutionalization put an end to this long and sometimes uneasy cohabitation. It is for this reason that the birth of a cinematic viewing style and of the "classical spectator" should not be separated from the attempt finally to offer the projector a room of its own. According to historians, the first buildings constructed as regular venues for projections date back to 1906–07—even if each country has its own chronology, and in Europe they tried to restructure pre-existing spaces whenever possible, especially in the city center. The big step was in any case already taken. With entirely new or partially modified architectural spaces, cinema had ceased to be a guest and could finally set the rules of the game in absolute freedom—invent for itself a viewing style that fully corresponded not only to what it was, but primarily to what it planned to become. This process was well described by Giuseppe Lavini in a 1918 article for *L'architettura italiana*: "The new institutions install themselves in suitable environments: then bit by bit as they take on their own shape, as they consolidate their own existence and establish the particulars of their functions, they set themselves up in buildings that have their own special form."

Some habits that the public contracted in the first years of the century would endure for quite a while. We know, for example, that, until the rise of the talkie, English spectators continued to divide themselves between the orchestra and balconies according to a convention typical of the music hall: those who planned to enjoy just a half-hour of entertainment watched from the orchestra, while those who intended to stay the entire evening went upstairs. However, with the birth of a place expressly conceived for movies, the hard part was already done. The compromises over, the solidarities of yesteryear renounced, compulsory cohabitation brought to an end, for cinema there suddenly opened a myriad of opportunities that had been unimaginable just a few years before.

Naturally, not even the dark cube came out of nowhere. Alongside the embarrassing relatives, others were, quite the contrary, worth keeping in contact with. The prose theatre that had so often generously hosted the first movie projections was one of these, and it should not come as a surprise that the architects charged with building a home for movies immediately adopted the playhouse as an obvious point of reference. Behind this choice, to be sure, there were precise technical motivations. Like the movie theatre, the "Italian playhouse"—which with its rigorous perspectival principles, rigid separation of stage and house, and framing of actors within the proscenium box is still the most diffuse type of theatrical building—placed its spectators directly facing the stage, and many of its schemes could be applied to the newcomer without effort. The proposal was successful, and the movie house's structure derives more or less from that model. However, excessive familiarity with the buildings born from this encounter must not lead us to take for granted the solution that won out, obscuring the importance but also the dramatic nature of the movies' exodus from "improvised viewing places" to "specialized structures" (terms that recall the passage from the outdoor, ambulatory spectacles of the Middle Ages to the first modern theatres).

No part of this process was easy or banal. On the contrary, the theatricalization of the venues must certainly be seen as part of a broader strategy of repositioning within the system of the arts, no less than were the analogy with the Platonic cave, or the adoption of classicizing formulae like "tenth muse" or "seventh art" to allude to cinema. It is quite probable, for instance, that the subdivision of seating by price range and the adoption of some architectural conventions of the past that were useless in the new context, like the curtain and the proscenium, served to make films seem familiar to the new, predominantly female and bour-geois, public. Siegfried Kracauer, moreover, had noted as far back as 1927 how the movie theatre's architectural frame was an integral part of a similar gentrification of cinema, and for this reason that it tended to "emphasize a dignity that used to inhabit the institutions of high culture. It favors the lofty and the *sacred* as if designed to promote works of eternal significance."

All of this is true. However, we must remember that the auditorium's principal objective was to impose on the audience a new attitude toward movies. The prose theatre meant a bourgeois public, but chiefly it meant particular viewing conditions. And it was here that architects' expertise came into play. The early cinema had been anything but a dark box, protected by the outside world and rigorously controlled in terms of its etiquette, which spectators from that moment on learned to associate with the idea of cinema. And yet it is only against the backdrop of this joyful chaos that we can understand the obsession with order and discipline that would spread in the following years. A bodiless eye, receptive to the stream of images, now had to take the place of the *eros*, the fear, and the desire that once lurked there in the darkness. Imitating the theatre, the dark cube in fact aspired to propose itself as a place of absolute aesthetic experience that allowed only one legitimate activity: the contemplation of a film.

The first task was to bar the doors to the chaos of the world outside; the rest would spontaneously follow. If spectators were going to watch the movie of the day with the same attention they gave to a live comedy or drama, it was essential that nothing prevented them from doing so. For this reason, the separation had to be both symbolic and real. Throughout the 1910s and '20s, movie professionals incessantly repeated the need to signal the border between the auditorium and the world outside. The point emerges almost obsessively in architects' writings and in press releases issued upon the opening of this or that picture palace. Indeed, we can hardly find a designer who did not insist upon the need for a majestic entrance that would psychologically prepare the spectator for the movie theatre's imaginary world. Nor do we lack detailed analyses of the psychological consequences of the wait for a film to begin. The most common strategy would, however, remain that of marking the separation from the outside world through luxury and extravagance, following the motto of American architect Charles Lee, designer of over 250 picture houses between 1920 and 1951: "The show starts on the sidewalk."

Neo-Greek, neo-Roman and neo-Egyptian, fake Venetian and fake Mexican, or fake Chinese and fake Indian: except for the neo-Gothic (too austere, and in Anglo-Saxon countries too tied to church and university architecture), any unusual style would do as long as it clearly told potential spectators that, crossing the threshold, they would enter an exotic land. As another American architect, Thomas Lamb, wrote,

> To make our audience receptive and interested, we must cut them off from the rest of the city life and take them into a rich and self-contained auditorium, where their minds are freed from the usual occupations and freed from their customary thoughts. In order to do this, it is necessary to present to their eyes a general scheme quite different from their daily environment, quite different in color scheme, and a great deal more elaborate.

At least until the 1929 stock market crash, there was no expedient or solution that architects had not tried in order to highlight this programmatic exceptionality: pilasters, windows, and towers accentuating the façade's verticality; imposing terracotta statues; monumental staircases; balustrades. And further: red carpets; chandeliers; bas-reliefs in a blaze of stuccos, marbles, and velvets, because nothing was too much if the objective was to stupefy the public and remind them that the movies had nothing to do with everyday life. The difference was to jump out at them, immediately. It hardly mattered that modernist architects and intellectuals derided the movie palace's "barbarous and suffocating magnificence," if hybridity and stylistic hodgepodge guaranteed that the theatre's doors would throw themselves open to reveal a whole other world.

In the end, even the enemies of "theme" buildings, supporters of a severe but not inelegant rationalism, underscored the uniqueness of the movie theatre in the urban space through a refusal of the traditional composite language, sometimes flanking the main body with a showy vertical structure, as in the most celebrated German movie houses of the 1920s, from the Universum to the Titania-Palast of Berlin, and later in the buildings of the British Odeon chain. This was a confirmation that—either through the combination of heterogeneous styles or instead through the elimination of extraneous detail—the dark cube needed to mark itself off unequivocally as an out-of-the-ordinary space, governed by laws and principles to which the audience needed to submit itself as soon as it crossed the threshold.

The history of twentieth-century cinema is also the history of this place and its precepts. As we have seen, the world of before, the world of the fairground cinema and cine-variety—permeable and vital—would disappear neither overnight nor without opposition or regrets. It was finally Al Jolson's voice in *The Jazz Singer* that would decree the end of the cinematic conviviality described by Delluc and other journalists of the epoch. October 6, 1927, naturally, can only be a symbolic date; and yet there is little doubt that, thanks to the advent of the sound film, in just a few years the early cinema's viewing style would be outmoded. The innovators' battle to regiment the public was long, but eventually won: a laborious process some ten years in the making was finally crowned sovereign when spectators were prohibited from moving and speaking during the film—not unlike what had happened in the playhouse. "Almost always silence": from that moment on, it would be imperative for the audience to watch only the images and nothing else, so that, as Cortázar has told us, looks could pour "onto the stage or the screen, fleeing from what's beside them, from what's on this side." The dark cube's epoch had begun.

3

Vitruvius's Sons

It so happens that human life in all its aspects, wide or narrow, is so intimately connected with architecture, that with a certain amount of observation we can usually reconstruct a bygone society from the remains of its public monuments. From relics of household stuff, we can imagine its owners "in their habit as they lived."

Honoré de Balzac, *The Quest of the Absolute*

As to the visual elements, the stage designer has a more powerful art at his disposal than the poet.

Aristotle, *The Poetics*

Through the definitive institutionalization of the dark cube, the history of the gaze came to know a rare moment of discontinuity. No expression we choose for the great caesura produced by the advent of the picture house (revolution? paradigm shift? rebirth?) could exaggerate the importance of the drift from one kind of spectator to another. Suddenly, going to the movies was like going to church: you sat composed, silent, immobile, completely committed to whatever happened on screen. Or at least cinema's new customers must have seemed this way in comparison to those who had gathered noisily in the back of a garage or in a vacant warehouse. It is not so relevant, then, that from this moment the history of the picture house was also—predictably—the history of the infractions against the stupendous effort to tightly control the public's behavior during the show. Seen from the 1920s, those transgressions appeared to be necessary exceptions to an irreversible trend that led the dark cube

quickly to impose its own viewing style just about everywhere, bulldoz-
ing over consolidated practices and definitively separating the history of
cinema from that of the *café-chantant*, the fair, and the variety stage.

It matters little that the process was inevitably partial, and that popular venues continued to house every kind of entertainment for quite a
while (in the early 1960s Jean-Luc Godard would still be in time to shoot
an Italian cine-variety in *Le mépris*). Though it is impossible to draw a
precise line between a "before" and an "after," with the rise of the movie
house and of the talkie the perception of what was normal and of what,
conversely, was suddenly no longer acceptable (moving around during
the film, commenting aloud about the scenes, entering and exiting the
house . . .) had simply changed. For good.

A cinematic architecture and new model of spectator emerged hand-
in-hand with a profound change in movies. Film historians agree: at least
until the early 1910s movies were so different from the entertainment we
know today that, strictly speaking, they should be treated as an autono-
mous form of expression with their own "language," to be understood
(and appreciated) in all its specificity. Herein lie the surprise and disappointment we experience when we approach the first short films: we
simply do not understand them. The mistake is of course our own,
because we ask them to resemble something that they are not, and did
not intend to be. But the feeling of absolute alterity such movies produce
today has stimulated research, and now we are in a better position to
comprehend that season, having finally renounced the idea of linear
evolution from simple to complex that dominated cinema histories until
a few decades ago.

Many of the films made prior to 1908 are simply "moving landscapes":
shots of the Gulf of Naples or the Forbidden City of Beijing. But when
an elementary plot takes shape, it corresponds only partly to our expectations, and we risk misinterpreting the image's meaning. It is not just
that close-up, aerial, and crane shots did not have the function they
would later acquire, for it is not even certain that the pioneers thought
about their works in the terms we do: for example, that they considered
them—under any profile—as "art." Generally speaking, their priorities
seem altogether different. In these works, the tension between punctual

and vectorial, image and sequence, framing and editing, that typifies later cinema is completely tilted in each case toward the first pole. From a formal point of view, the most conspicuous characteristic of this "cinema of attractions" (as scholars call it) is probably the short films' serial structure, internally organized as a sequence of highly spectacular numbers—the real "highlights" of the projection—often completely gratuitous with respect to the story's main action (when story exists) but appreciated by the public for their high visual impact.

Directors fought to avoid losing, even for an instant, the hold on the spectator, who literally needed to be kept attached to the seat. This was the first commandment of the original cinema, and even the movies' limited duration, which allowed for alternating diverse subjects and themes and offered new sensory stimuli, responded in the end to the same need. When the first feature-length films were distributed around 1910, a cinematic spectacle must have seemed like little more than an uninterrupted, rapid, random sequence of comedy sketches, newsreels, magic acts, moving landscapes, and short adaptations of great literary classics (from Shakespeare to Dante, from Victor Hugo to the *Little Flowers of St Francis*).

This similarity to the variety stage's poetics of shock, created by juxtaposing heterogeneous material, reconfirms the primitive cinema's chameleonic readiness to adapt itself to the entertainments that, in those difficult years, hosted it for an evening or two. From the very beginning, films were regularly inserted into café-concert or music hall programs; and there were plenty who, like futurist Filippo Tommaso Marinetti in the 1913 *Variety Theatre Manifesto*, looked to film as a precious resource for innovating performance with "an incalculable number of otherwise unrealizable visions and spectacles (battles, riots, races, automobile and airplane circuits, trips, transatlantic flights, the depths of cities, the countryside, oceans, and skies)."

Developments would show that what seemed to many a love match was in reality a marriage of convenience; but years would pass before cinema renounced the errors of its youth. How to fault the futurists—at least on this level? The first films seemed conceived precisely for the time between a singer's number and a musician's act. Fragmentary,

incoherent, brief, easy to follow for their simple plots and weak character psychologies, these movies were absolutely perfect for a cinema that
had not yet discovered the centripetal force of the house. The music
hall's viewing style allowed people to chat, glancing occasionally at the
screen without necessarily following the story, or, by the same token, to
choose to let the calculated rhythm of the images carry them away. In
either case, none of cinema's pleasures would be lost.

When the first great directors—Giovanni Pastrone, David W.
Griffith, Louis Feuillade, Victor Sjöström, Stellan Rye, and other celluloid pioneers like them—appeared in the 1910s, the alliance between
cinema and the variety stage reached a crisis point. It is certainly no acci-
dent that the change in the viewing style favored by the first permanent
picture houses (from 1906 to 1907) substantially coincided with the rise
of the narrative (1908–09) and feature-length (1912–13) film. The new
movies required a completely novel code of spectator conduct, and only
a radical theatricalization of the spaces seemed to reassure directors who
wished to experiment with the new art's potential. We do not necessarily
need to establish a cause-and-effect relationship between these phenomena, but we ought not to ignore their synchrony. In the mid 1910s films
had begun to ask spectators for increasingly complete dedication, to the
point of claiming the entire stay inside the venue and discouraging any
alternative activities, marginalizing and finally deposing the attractions
with which they had formerly shared spaces and audiences.

Of course, a metamorphosis of such rapidity and scope was not a
foregone conclusion. In this process, the Italian playhouse became a
precious—indeed, irreplaceable—resource at the service of a renewed
viewing style. Separating light from dark and imposing silent immobility on spectators, the dark cube offered a decisive hand to a narrative
cinema of increasingly complex plots. Without it, the rise of the new
films—which were longer and more sophisticated than ever before—
would have been slower and more difficult, maybe even impossible.

Aesthetic devices are never neutral, and the dark cube is no exception.
Rather, what is striking is the staying power and resistance of the primitive viewing style. A winding road, not without contradictory signs,
would in fact open up in the middle of the 1910s. The two cinemas would

coexist until the advent of the talkies without one completely unseating the other; and even later, the other viewing style would not disappear entirely, coming at least partially back to life each time architecture loosened its constrictive grip on the public—almost as if the process triggered by the picture house were always about to change course.

In just a few short years the dark cube provoked stylistic and thematic renovation. Considering the intensity of the objections against multireel films, we might suspect that, without the movie house, narrative cinema would not have been so quickly accepted. Journals of the period overflow with articles worriedly denouncing the feature-length film's pretense to constructing elaborate stories in imitation of novels or plays. Aniello Costagliola, an Italian playwright and journalist who took up film criticism in 1908, wrote for *Cinema* in 1912: "It's an outright disaster! Long films have taken over the cinema!" Of course, such cries were not the only response, and in fact critics typically held positions of compromise, for instance observing that in principle "the feature-length film ought to be an exception for those works that are really worth developing thousands of meters of film" (this an anonymous journalist from *La Vita Cinematografica* in January of 1914). The tone is different, yet the sense of these testimonies is fundamentally the same: on the eve of the Great War, proposing a program entirely centered on a single multireel movie could have been risky for a proprietor who, taking for granted a lukewarm public response, felt obliged to concoct a series of strategies to counterbalance the monotony of shows that were too long. The range of interventions could vary enormously from film to film, and depended only on the imagination and means of their executors. Live actors dressing "in theme," fountains gushing colored water, choral interludes, light displays: in the most elegant houses, nothing was too excessive to help spectators digest a film lasting an hour and a half or two—a length then considered almost intolerable.

The first viewing styles would not disappear from one day to the next. In the 1930s, for example, the Italian press continued to print lamentations that cinema was "reduced to being a complement to the variety stage": a clear indication that its closeness to light entertainment (including the possibility of using the camera to record the performance of a

particularly talented performer and show it elsewhere) endured longer
than is normally stated. For quite some time after the talkie's arrival, many
theatres continued to use films as part of a bigger show, alternating the
attractions to provide a miscellaneous program that allocated on average
one-fourth to one-third of the evening to live acts. In short, the *café-chantant* formula, which offered a movie too, dominated for quite some
time—as is suggested by the objections of the new art's enthusiasts (like
Kracauer) against the coupling of variety numbers or comic sketches with
projections. Almost as if the film on its own were not enough.

  This difficulty in casting off the variety cinema and its viewing style
requires us to resist any teleological reading of the great transformation. The "cinema of attractions" not only represented one particularly
tenacious kind of show, but also continued to boast many admirers
among those who came along in time to get to know it and never
stopped grieving for it—especially the avant-garde writers who saw in
its lack of intellectual pretense a potential ally against bourgeois art.
There are many possible examples, but one in particular is worth
dwelling on: Walter Benjamin. Between 1935 and 1936, in writing
"The Work of Art in the Age of Mechanical Reproduction," surely
one of the most commented-on but also most misunderstood essays of
the twentieth century, Benjamin wondered how the new technical arts
were transforming aesthetics. Here he devised the celebrated theory of
the "loss of aura" in a world of copies in which the very notion of
originality, with cinema and photography, had entered into permanent
crisis. The text is particularly relevant for a discussion of the movie
house, because in its second, least-read part, Benjamin credited the
film with having forever transformed our relationship to the work of
art, imposing on spectators a new conduct characterized by—as he
wrote—"simultaneous collective experience" and "reception in a state
of distraction" (*Zerstreuung*). This second issue is the one that concerns
us (the first, more traditional, is in fact also valid for theatre). Already
in 1907, Italian writer Giovanni Papini had noted the new art's peculiarity, which, unlike a painting, novel, or opera, "does not demand too
much culture, too much attention, too much effort to keep up with it."
Benjamin (who did not cite and most likely had not read Papini) takes

this intuition to extreme conclusions: films would be conceived expressly for negligent spectators open to being captured by the images only in some fragmentary way. All these factors would liken the cinematic experience to the superficial enjoyment people take from architecture as they wander about the city: "Reception in a state of distraction, which is increasingly noticeable in all fields of art and is symptomatic of profound changes in apperception, finds in the film its true means of exercise . . . The public is an examiner, but an absentminded one."

If one reads "The Work of Art" in parallel with the essays Benjamin dedicated to Bertolt Brecht in the same period, the similarities with his descriptions of epic theatre might lead one to conclude that cinema interested Benjamin mainly as a spontaneously Brechtian medium ("the concept of the epic theater . . . indicates above all that this theater desires an audience that is relaxed and follows the action without strain"). This is hardly odd: the Benjamin–Brecht relationship is a canonical topic of philosophy and of German literary studies. However, no one emphasizes enough that the movies Benjamin identified as a new art for the masses were not the feature-length films of the 1930s, with elaborate stories and strong narrative cohesion, but the short sketches (comic and otherwise) of the 1910s and, already much less, of the 1920s. When Benjamin wrote in 1935–36, those movies simply no longer played, and the new picture houses had some time ago supplanted the promiscuous spaces described by Delluc. Of course, the films' irreversible transformation did not prevent Benjamin from nostalgically looking back, as he had done in *Berlin Childhood* with the legendary "Kaiserpanorama." So, not unlike the other great German theorists of the 1930s, when Benjamin composed his seminal essay, he continued to think of silent film. But while in the same years Bela Balázs, Rudolph Arnheim, and Erwin Panofsky mourned the late expressionist or Soviet masterpieces—victoriously compared to the first miserable attempts at filmed theatre—the author of *Angelus Novus* missed completely different movies: single-reel stories, slapstick comedies, newsreels. Films, that is to say, perfectly enjoyable by sample or fragment and better adapted to the variety hall or fair. After all, a cryptic affirmation like "at the movies [the position of critic] requires no attention" makes sense only in reference to that kind of work.

Benjamin's resistance is probably the best testimony to the new cinema's difficulty in being accepted, not only in the most radical avant-garde milieu. Benjamin himself, though, would quickly realize that the "cinema of attractions" had lost its battle. His famous December 1938 letter to Adorno about "The Work of Art" should be read as a retraction generated not so much by the desire to please his friend as by the bitter awareness that those films, those venues, and those spectators simply no longer existed: "I see more and more clearly that the launching of the sound film must be regarded as an operation of the film industry designed to break the revolutionary primacy of the silent film, which has produced reactions that were difficult to control and hence dangerous politically." Talkies had hurried along a process underway at least since the middle of the previous decade; but, as a result, the art that according to Benjamin illustrated the new relationship between artist and his public in the age of technical reproducibility suddenly found itself relegated to the past, in a condition much like the enchanted objects of his childhood. As always, the Benjaminian utopia—aesthetic no less than political—is intensely regressive.

In light of recent research, it is now difficult to contest the tie binding the metamorphosis of movies, conditions of projection, and viewing style. All three began at the same moment, between 1910 and 1915, even if the process required more time for the theatres and the public. A new type of film implicated a new model of spectator and a new aesthetic device—the dark cube—most capable of enhancing directors' efforts. But of course the reverse was also true: the completely novel device seemed designed specifically to support those experiments, favoring the evolution toward plots with a complexity unimaginable just a few years before. However this relationship is articulated, the birth of classical cinema (with its precepts and its characteristic "Institutional Mode of Representation": the identification of the viewer's perspective with a ubiquitous camera, continuity editing, spatial and temporal consistency, and so on) was inseparable from the invention of the classical spectator—the spectator who views the film perfectly still and silent in the darkness of the house. As we do yet today when we go to the movies.

Here, too, a parallel with the appearance of the Italian playhouse in sixteenth-century Europe may be useful. In the Renaissance, the desire to find a non-ephemeral space for spectators went hand-in-hand with the idea of recouping a type of work very different from the religious dramas and street farces of medieval theatre. The new repertory of comedies and tragedies proposed by the humanists enjoyed the prestige of lost antiquity, but staging a spectacle in the manner of the Greeks and Romans was a risky bet all the same. Even if Plautus, Terence, and Seneca were widely studied in grammar schools, their success on stage could not be taken for granted. Tightly knit plots, complex character psychologies, elevated language not always easily understood by an audience that was neither entirely literate nor accustomed to such shows: How would spectators respond? There was real danger of "losing" a public called to confront, for the first time after about a thousand years, the works of the ancients or their imitators who composed in blank verse, alexandrines, and free hendecasyllables.

The anecdote told by a contemporary reporter—that Plautus's *Miles Gloriosus* triumphed in Venice in February 1515 only thanks to the clowns' comic interludes—speaks volumes. Who could guarantee that the shows would be comprehensible and, more importantly, trigger the catharsis that Aristotle had taught was the purpose of tragedy? Concerns all the more understandable if we consider that staging Greek and Roman plays meant giving up one of the most potent factors intensifying the aesthetic experience: the organic link with ritual and liturgy from which medieval religious dramas benefited.

For the men who began to alternate reading and commentary with new staging practice for the first time in centuries, there were pitfalls everywhere. Turning to the classics, seeking to transform Sophocles and Euripides into a living repertory meant advancing into uncharted terri-tories. The results of such a mission, moreover, were far from guaranteed. If Aristotle had seen "purgation" as the spontaneous response to a particular type of aesthetic solicitation (according to the general claim by which tragedy "through pity and fear effects the proper purgation of these emotions"), sixteenth-century authors tended to think of it as the result of considerable effort, only some of which was intrinsically connected to plot and versification. In all likelihood, the moderns' obsession with catharsis (which Aristotle liquidated in two lines, but Trissino, Castelvetro, Robortello, Piccolomini, and Segni transformed into the fulcrum of Aristotelean theatrical theory) is closely tied to the fear of failing to activate the dramaturgical mechanism.

The theatrical experiments of the 1500s are incomprehensible if we do not keep this uncertainty in mind. And this should not be all that surprising. Without a doubt, the classic texts were more difficult, even in translation. Any unforeseen event would be enough to shatter the mimesis and irreversibly compromise the spectators' involvement. And since no single detail could be left to chance, it was precisely in the face of this threat of utter failure that the architectural science of the ancients, and of Vitruvius in particular, offered a precious contribution.

Only the worst kind of scholarly specialization has made it possible to treat Vitruvius's recuperation and Aristotle's renewed circulation as two independent events. We remember all too rarely, for example, that Andrea Palladio, the designer of the first permanent theatre of the Renaissance (the Teatro Olimpico in Vicenza, Italy, 1585), spent his formative years in the circles of Giangiorgio Trissino, one of the key figures in the diffusion of the *Poetics*, not to mention the author of the first classicist tragedy, *The Sofonisba* (in 1515). From then on, reflections on Vitruvius and Aristotle, on drama and on places of performance, ran parallel; and the acquisition of the ancient repertory coincided with the rediscovery (in reality, the invention) of a building for performances. In all of these authors—the Leon Battista Albertis, the Pellegrino Priscianis, the Sebastiano Serlios, the Giovan Battista Giraldi Cinzios, the Leone de' Sommis, the Angelo Ingegneris—the desire to recuperate the Greek and Roman theatre as universal experience (the same dream that led to the creation of the opera at the beginning of the 1600s) is accompanied by the fear that tragedies and comedies would for the moderns be condemned to silent reading. The text was not enough, the actors were not enough, the plotting was not enough, the music was not enough. Something in addition to the scenic fiction was needed, and Renaissance men of the theatre hoped that this something could come from a building expressly conceived as a giant spectacle machine capable of breaking the public's resistance. In order for the spell to materialize, the space created to house the performance would have to follow the lesson of the ancients.

The stakes were much higher than the successful outcome of this or that single show. For Renaissance humanists, educating the public in the classical theatre was part of a much more comprehensive project of re-creating man in the likeness of the Greeks and Romans. Euripides and Terence asked the sixteenth century's spectators to watch and listen like the ancients did—*to be moved as they were*—just as treatises on etiquette told them they should imitate the ancients' mode of riding horseback, dressing, or dining at table. Simply put, like eloquence and good manners, catharsis was to be gained through proper pedagogical training. The fifth book of *De architectura* taught how to build a Roman theatre, obtain perfect acoustics, and shield spectators from the sun or from the stench of unwholesome quarters. But above all Vitruvius's pages would lead to an idea of spectacle radically opposed to the one that dominated throughout the Middle Ages.

The importance of the question would become increasingly clear for those men of the theatre educated according to the precepts of ancient culture. In the ten books of Leon Battista Alberti's *De re aedificatoria*, completed between 1443 and 1452, the architect's only task was to put the spectators in a condition to see and hear effortlessly what was happening on stage (in particular, good acoustics and a large stage had to compensate for the particular makeup of Roman structures, where actors played further back and not in the orchestra, as in Greece). However, over time new considerations would enrich both theorists' reflections and performances of ancient drama. As the century progressed and experiments diversified, faith in the house's psychagogic potential increased. In a cross between old and new, many suggestions that seemed derived from the ancients were elaborated day by day in response to the concrete difficulties of putting on a play; but the desire for an art that regulated passions through emotional participation would remain unabashedly Aristotelean. Raked stage, perspective scenery (where actors had to play on the forestage to avoid shattering the illusion of depth), strict separation of the completely dark house from the marvelously illuminated stage (by means of the proscenium arch and the curtain): in the course of the sixteenth century we see a multiplication of the strategies that, if followed precisely, would make it impossible for the public to reject the fiction offered to them.

Some recommendations seem quite reasonable, even obvious, five centuries later, like the age-old polemic against *intermezzi* that were too long and thus threatened to interrupt the drama's logic and wholeness. Other concerns can seem to us a bit more extravagant, but they make sense within a poetics of total mimesis like Aristotle's. One such fear is that the actors would not match the scenery and would therefore reveal the illusion; this worry was translated into an invitation to avoid painting live beings unless in a state of slumber. For instance, Sebastiano Serlio, in *The Second Book of Architecture* (1545) wrote that

> some artists are in the habit of painting living characters in these scenes—such as a woman on a balcony or in a doorway, even a few animals. I do not recommend this practice, however, because although the figures represent living creatures they show no movement. On the other hand, it is quite appropriate to represent some person who sleeps, or some dog or other animal that sleeps, because no movement is expected here.

But instead of dwelling on single stratagems—which would take us too far off-course—let us consider the logic underpinning the entire operation. The sixteenth century is full of treatises written by architects, set designers, and mathematicians teaching how to vanquish spectator resistance through an adequate management of the scenic space. A main characteristic of Renaissance Italy's theatrical reform was in fact this absolute, unprecedented faith in the ability of buildings to influence the public's reaction. Yet it would be difficult to speak of optimism, as we are wont to do with these men of letters who were so ready to celebrate the end of the Dark Ages and the rebirth of classical culture. An additional contribution was asked of architecture precisely because spectators were so ill inclined to be captivated, and any little triviality sufficed to interrupt the flow of emotions and compromise the show. Reading between the lines, it is as if Renaissance thespians were united in the common fear of failing to create convincing illusions, of not having done everything possible to ensure that the fiction finally got the best of disbelief. The abundance of the solutions they proposed is a sign of insecurity and not—as we would more logically suspect—of faith in the possibility of seeing *in the manner of the ancients*.

The beginnings of the Italian playhouse allow us to understand some of the reasons architects would turn to it four centuries later in order to give cinema a permanent home. In their quest, the same events seem to repeat themselves. We find an identical pessimism with regard to the public's readiness to accept a work so different from those that had circulated until then. With long and complex narratives, the films that appeared in the mid 1910s required a new kind of attention, just as Renaissance classicist drama had. The original venues no longer corresponded to the movies that directors strained to impose upon an audience reluctant to go along with their experiments. Exactly as Renaissance theoreticians had sought help in "constructing the spectator" through architecture, the narrative cinema also demanded a receptivity and vigilance that only the auditorium's rituals and prohibitions could assure. On their own, the camera and the projector were sufficient to film a scene and bring it back to life, but if a director aspired to do more than give spectators the impression that moving landscapes were real (if for example he hoped to tell a story through images, as happened increasingly often), these machines risked no longer being enough. And here architecture proffered a solution, promising to discipline a public otherwise too inclined to succumb to a thousand distractions.

Too little thought has been given to the fact that cinema has not one but two apparently contradictory myths of origin. The most famous—everyone knows it—centers on the very first projection at the Café des Capucines, when people fled the auditorium for fear of being run over by the image of the train entering the La Ciotat station. The story is without historical credence, but is nonetheless significant, inspired as it is by cinema's pride in the illusionary power of its technology. The second myth is also frequently recalled by silent film theorists, even though it is no more tenable. It hinges on a European who has lived at length in Africa, or a peasant from the far reaches of Siberia, who encounters cinema for the first time and, unable to comprehend editing's basic principles, confuses close-ups for unlikely conversations between severed heads—a dysphoric rather than euphoric and Promethean myth this time; an admission of weakness and of a relationship with the public that presents no problem when the scope is simply to represent reality but will encounter unforeseen obstacles as soon as the film attempts to elevate its status to that of Art. "We ourselves no longer know by what intricate evolution of our consciousness we have learned our visual association of ideas," commented Bela Balázs after joyfully retelling a series of such anecdotes.

Inasmuch as we are talking about foundational myths, it hardly matters that experimental studies have shown that we do not actually need a special code to decipher films. What is interesting in this case is that the distance between the two stories could not be greater, nor the opposition between their morals more absolute. Suspended between approaching train and severed heads conversing—between too much and too little—cinema never gets to choose just one myth, and instead oscillates from knowledge of its own power to an equally strong recognition of the difficulty in obtaining the total faith of its audience. And here, before the threat of spectator incomprehension, the theatre (a place, but also a symbol of artistic legitimacy) comes into play. The adoption of the auditorium responded to a different but complementary need: to bring the viewing styles of cinema and theatre closer together so as to elicit from the public the same attention it devoted to plays, without neglecting those who had never been to the prose theatre and were ready to become the phalanx of contrite, orderly, and silent spectators required by the new filmic narratives.

An entirely theatricalized cinema necessarily called for a wholly theatrical space. Of course this *imitatio theatri* was subject to many diverse interpretations, according to the different senses of the word. Theatre as a noble art? Theatre as a synonym for complex plots and character psychologies? Theatre as a place of performance? The slippage from one meaning to another is frequent in texts of the period, but the architectural issue retains its own specificity. Thus, if we move from the France of Delluc and Epstein and the Italy of Papini and Marinetti to, for example, Weimar Germany, we find a unique proto-cinephile like Fred Hood (pseudonym of the secondary school principal Friedrich Huth), and read passages such as this:

> When we enter into a movie house, we immediately see the screen on the wall, which is nothing other than a large cloth framed with wood or velvet. We know that on this cloth nothing can really happen, as it were; it is as if it lacks the stage to put a good number of people in the scene. We would like to fall under the illusion, but this ought not to be made so difficult for us. Entering the auditorium, for example, we expect to see a stage. It is incredible how our emotions rise when, taking our place, we find the familiar old stage and curtain; certainly, the curtain should cover only the screen, hiding its edges. But our fancy enchants us, and we imagine a complete set design with wings, dressing rooms, trapdoors, machines that put actors in flight, etc. If one does not want to construct an artificial stage, there is still another possibility for intensifying the illusion. An architectural frame can be placed on the wall to make the screen seem to emerge from a big opening. In this way we would see the events, as it were, from the balcony of a salon, from a castle loggia. This seems like an even better solution because we get something like the impression that everything is happening far away. Anyone who keeps these elements in mind will manage greatly to increase the public's interest in movies.

This quotation is a bit long, but it underscores a common attitude among the first cinema enthusiasts, when the film was still thought of essentially as an instrument for recording and disseminating a previous theatrical performance. Not everyone, of course, shared this position, and opposing ideas would soon emerge among the most innovative architects. The Viennese Frederick Kiesler, for example, who designed the futuristic Film Guild Theatre of New York in 1928, argued that while "the cinema is a play of surfaces, the theatre is a performance in space, and this difference has not yet been translated concretely into any piece of architecture, neither for the theatre nor for the cinema." According to Kiesler, new picture houses needed to depart from this elementary difference. "The most important quality of an auditorium" for films was in fact the "ability to suggest concentrated attention that at the same time destroys the sensation of containment easily produced when the spectator rests his eyes on the screen," putting him in a condition to "lose himself in an infinite imaginary space." A position totally contrary to Huth's, in other words. Kiesler would in fact specify a few years later that "the first decisive step toward the creation of an ideal movie theatre is the abolition of the proscenium and of every other element that reminds one of the stage of a theatre." But here we are already at the end of the 1920s, when film could claim a stable position in the system of the arts. The Italian playhouse model having solidly established itself, the need became that of vindicating the dark cube's particularity with respect to its sixteenth-century ancestors. After all, cinema wanted to be the art of modernity *par excellence*—a dream that in years to come would inspire the visionary Kiesler to design a space where images were projected on the side walls and ceiling as well.

Today Fred Hood's worries might make us chuckle, but actually they are the surest measure of the belief, then quite widespread, that only in going toward theatre—imitating it in *all* its aspects—would cinema express itself to its full potential. This was obviously not Benjamin's opinion; for him, if anything, theatre should have emulated cinema, as in Brecht's epic theatre, where organizing the story by fragments and eliminating the separation between stage and house seemed to respond to the goal of conforming to the new art ("Like the pictures in a film, epic theatre moves in spurts. Its basic form is that of the shock with which the single, well-defined situations of the play collide"). But, as we know, Benjamin pinned the future of art in the age of its infinite reproducibility on its reception in a state of distraction. In contrast, Fred Hood—like many of his contemporaries and the directors who were not closely tied to the avant-garde—aspired to reinforce the kinship with theatre's dramaturgical traditions: to make cinema above all a narrative art capable of telling stories, even if through images. The adoption of the Italian playhouse model, for all practical purposes, was integral to this process.

The best intuitions on the auditorium's function in cinema's economy of make believe probably come from architects or cross-disciplinary figures who, like Peter Greenaway, undertook architectural studies in their youth and were thus predisposed to give due attention to the public's material conditions. Reading their reflections alongside those of Leon Battista Alberti or Pellegrino Prisciani makes more explicit some of the characteristics of the cinematic apparatus that might go unobserved if we read only the twentieth-century texts. In fact, by comparison with the authors of the 1500s, the architects of the 1920s offer us just fragments of a formulation that becomes truly comprehensible only against the backdrop of the first great battle for the Vitruvian spectator.

A discussion of the picture house centered on the spectator's concrete, physical experience must begin here. The awareness that they were designing spaces that would elicit a precise emotive response from spectators offered architects a powerful antidote to the shortcuts of psychoanalysis and the false analogy with dreaming. An architect knows—must know—that people do not go to the movies to sleep, but to attend a show. It is therefore rather strange (and a little disappointing) that Kracauer, who had a degree in architecture, would have brilliant intuitions in the 1920s and then later, during his American period, fall back on an all-too-conventional theory of film as hypnosis of the masses. Naturally, it is possible that some of the architects' solutions will disappoint us, partly because, as we have already seen, a fundamental unity of approach would not at all translate into uniform results. If some of their judgments seem immediately sensible (like the insistence on the entrance's decisive function), others might appear more naïve when not outright bizarre, like the declared need for a frame and a curtain tying cinema back to theatre (this is Friederich Huth's position). However, none of these particular judgments count for much when we consider that what is important here is not any isolated suggestion, but the general acknowledgement of the psychological ends of architecture and its ability to control perception.

Called to design spaces fit for this task, architects like Giuseppe Lavini, Thomas Lamb, Charles Lee, and Frederick Kiesler, or architecture critics like Philip Morton Shand, were in the best position to appreciate how every single element of the dark cube—from the inclination of the seats to the format of the screen, from the masking of light to illumination—contributed to the final effect. But most of their guiding principles were simple adaptations of the laws formulated by their sixteenth-century predecessors. In some cases, the similarity between the reflections of cinema's first theorists and the precepts of Renaissance architects is really striking. When, for example, the young Kracauer attacks the mixing of live performance and film in a single show with the argument that "by its very existence, film demands that the world it reflects be the only one," and that for this reason "it should be wrested from every three-dimensional surrounding lest it fail as an illusion," at first we might think we are reading a slightly updated version of Serlio's warning that the proximity of live beings on painted sets to flesh-and-blood would provoke the spectator's disbelief, and therefore the failure of the performance.

For our purposes, the crucial points regarding the Italian playhouse are two. First, through the auditorium, cinema borrowed from theatre a radically different viewing style. Second, and most importantly, a particular kind of film—narrative feature-length movies—found in the auditorium an ideal companion, in a manner not unlike what happened 400 years earlier with classicist drama.

The inverse is also true. Precisely because places of performance corresponded to a certain type of representation for so long, around the same time that cineastes sought to give projections a room of their own, theatre's greatest innovators—from George Fuchs to Gordon Craig, from Jacques Copeau to Max Reinhardt—rejected the Italian playhouse's confines. It was almost as if, after Wagner, a true director or playwright had to be, at least a little, also an architect. To free oneself from the Vitruvian tradition—to free oneself from Alberti, from Serlio, from Ingegneri, from Palladio—in their case meant bidding farewell to an idea of theatre whose font of inspiration seemed dried up. It was time to start anew: if necessary, to return to myth and to the sacred dimensions of the most ancient forms of spectacle (Aristotle, significantly, spoke of tragedy without a single reference to the religious framing of the performances). Whereas, for opposite reasons, cinema hoped to reoccupy the theatre's spaces, to retrieve their wisdom, and maybe even to inherit their public.

Seen in this context, the theatricalization of cinema's viewing style turns out to be a decisive event in the history of twentieth-century art. In the end, things were not so different with painting when photography—having taken up its mimetic imperative—released it from the "mummy complex" afflicting it since the Renaissance. "Photography," André Bazin wrote many years ago in a now classic essay, "is clearly the most important event in the history of the plastic arts. Simultaneously a liberation and a fulfillment, it has freed Western painting, once and for all, from its obsession with realism and allowed it to recover its aesthetic autonomy." The impulse to adapt this notion to the relationship between cinema and theatre is irresistible. The Lumière brothers' invention was an extremely powerful incentive for avant-garde theatre directors engaged in the search for an art that drew from ritual sources and—in open revolt against naturalism—recovered an entirely symbolic conception of the scenic space, achieving a return to origins that seemed suddenly to close an almost four-century-long parenthesis. This was perhaps similar to what Balázs had predicted since the 1920s, rejoicing that, in regard to theatre,

> because it can no longer compete with cinema on this terrain, it has abandoned the attempt to furnish a faithful image of nature. The obligation to achieve *vraisemblance* is in any case one that theatre had long since denied itself and lost from view. Instead, it reduced its ambition to rendering as faithfully as possible the passive scene of the action.

Film, he argued, citing Tairov, "'unshackled' the theatre." From the moment when the theatrical avant-garde turned its back on the Italian playhouse, declaring war on the bourgeois public, cinema went in the opposite direction and launched a conquest of new spectators who were until then little familiar with the world of Hecuba and Berenice (partly due to high ticket prices). For this reason, only a parallel reading of the two phenomena will enable us to grasp the broader implications of this comprehensive redefinition of the arts that took place in the first decades of the twentieth century.

However, as we have seen, this is not enough. Alongside this brief timeline (roughly speaking, the period from 1895 to 1930), we must not forget the longer one (from the sixteenth century to the twentieth century). The breakthrough of a cinema increasingly inseparable from the dark cube can in fact be fully understood only against the backdrop of the classicist drama's move toward a permanent theatrical building. In the history of the gaze, the movie house's institutionalization simply represents the second step of a single process of aesthetic disciplining and education of that gaze—a phenomenon very similar, but this time destined to reach social sectors that had previously been strangers to even the boulevard theatres: men, but also women and children, now forced to follow an entire behavioral code in order to appreciate the story unfolding before them.

The film historians who rediscovered the show's first forms were sometimes rather severe about the passage to the Italian playhouse and the adoption of an intensely theatrical viewing style. For some of them, adhering to the bourgeois theatre's codes meant curtailing the public's freedom of expression and normalizing the "public sphere" (this was the thesis, above all, of Miriam Hansen). Such a judgment contains an element of truth. There is no doubt, for example, that the dark cube—as an aesthetic device capable of conditioning the reactions of spectators and forcing them to watch a film in the "right way"—reproduces in an artistic ambit the project of an epoch obsessed with the rise of the masses and determined to control their reawakening. Even among architects, conventionally paternalistic pronouncements about the popular classes abound; they often speak explicitly of the luxury of the new theatres as a means for domesticating the working class and halting the clamor for reforms from below. "No king or emperor has ever wandered through more sumptuous places than this. In a sense these locales are a social safety valve, for the public can partake in the same luxuries as the rich," wrote Harold Rambush, an esteemed American decorator from the golden age of the movie palace. Echoing his sentiment on the other side of the Atlantic was the condescending judgment of Theodor Komisarjevsky, the Russian émigré who quickly became the chief designer of movie houses in the England of the 1920s:

> The richly decorated theatre, the comfort with which they are surrounded, the efficiency of the service contribute to an atmosphere and a sense of well-being of which the majority have hitherto only dreamed. While there they can with reason consider themselves as good as anyone, and are able to enjoy their cigarettes or their little love affairs in comfortable seats and amidst attractive and appealing surroundings.

In short, *panem et circenses*.

But perhaps it is possible to see the same phenomenon from a different perspective. Not every act of discipline is a form of education, but all educative processes (even of an aesthetic nature) require an irrefutable dose of constraint and violence. Neither the Italian playhouse nor its more fortunate descendent, the movie house, are exceptions. The theatricalization of cinematic spaces from the start favored the diffusion of a new kind of movie, much more complex than those that had circulated until that moment: films requiring a public intensely receptive for their duration, and films putting within everyone's reach an aesthetic experience based on tenets similar to those of the great Western dramatic tradition.

The two aspects were closely connected. Griffith's pretense to being the Dickens of the new art was not entirely unfounded, but he would never have been able to conceive of projects like *Intolerance* or *Birth of a Nation* if movies had not already decisively set off down theatre's path. We must not forget, in short, that only the Vitruvian edifice had made possible the qualitative leap through which cinema became the art we know. However unconsciously, the dark cube was maybe the last heir of that humanistic dream that viewed the Italian playhouse as crucial to the

restoration and dissemination of the ancients' lifestyle among the
moderns: an (aesthetic) utopia of man's complete rebirth by disciplining
the emotions that cinema all of a sudden found itself promoting—
democratically—beyond the humanists' most optimistic expectations.

It is important to be clear on one point. The dark cube not only
accompanied the new films in their first steps, but also facilitated the rise
of a different form of pleasure than movies had previously offered.
Before the establishment of the Vitruvian structure and of feature-length
films, cinema audiences' passions held little in common with those of
theatregoers. Even without insisting too much on the contraposition of
visual and narrative elements (an old critical distinction that recent
research suggests should be blurred), the first movies were dominated
by a taste for surprise and wonder tightly connected to the aesthetic
device's portentous illusionistic capacity. With respect to this phase, in
which satisfaction was tied to the medium's ability to show something
impossible (Méliès), or to show spectators, almost as if they were present,
something that had happened elsewhere (Lumière), the arrival of the
feature-length narrative film radically changed the nature of entertainment, teasing and satisfying other desires closer to those that had brought
the public to the theatre: vicissitudes, adventures, recognitions, *coups de
théâtre*, races against time, and especially the pleasure of suffering and
rejoicing with and for a character as if for an old friend.

Something is always lost in such major transformations. Even for
theatre, the process was far from simple, and only partially successful.
Accounts from the eighteenth century—when the polemic against the
immorality of theatrical spectacle raged from Paris to Venice—are full
of truly appalling descriptions, and they depict a situation that could not
be further from the actor–spectator cooperation the writings of the
sixteenth-century Italian architects would lead us to expect. According
to Richard Sennett, only in the second half of the nineteenth century,
along with a radical metamorphosis of the relationship between individual and society, did spectators begin to practice the self-control we
take for granted at any theatrical performance and avoid expressing
aloud their approval or disapproval of what was happening on stage.

The reality is always less monolithic and more malleable than the abstract models into which every theory (beginning with sixteenth-century Italian Aristotelean ones) would like to fit it. The thousands of infractions against the code—gleaned from just a few pages of Denis Diderot on the conditions of Parisian spectacle—did not prevent cinema from looking to theatre as a prestigious model or change the fact that its migration toward the Italian playhouse would have aesthetically (if not politically) revolutionary consequences. Films extended the same educational program to a much vaster audience for the first time: an audience whose access to the temples of dramatic art had been limited, and that was now slowly being led to participate in new ways and—if we want to give credence to myth one last time—to learn the difference between a dialogue in close-up and a conversation among severed heads. From that moment on, the dark cube's principal task would be to "construct," by force of prohibition and prescription, the spectators Griffith and Pastrone needed in order to tell their stories. That is exactly what Vitruvius's sons were there for.

4

The Age of Freedom

Motion pictures are entering their third major era. First there was the silent period. Then the sound era. Now we are on the threshold of the television age.

Samuel Goldwyn (1949)

[T]he nature of the audience of an art, its particular mode of participation and perception, is internal to the nature of that art.

Stanley Cavell, *The World Viewed*

A successful imitation is always an imperfect imitation—partial, in its own way incomplete. The history of the relationship between the movie theatre and the playhouse does not seem to escape this elementary principle. For instance, the new picture palaces had no need of dressing rooms, so all that backstage space was suddenly useless; but the Italian playhouse's entire scheme was to be placed in the service of the cinematic technology and viewing style that were partly different from, even if closely inspired by, those of the lyric and prose theatres.

Once again—it should come as no surprise—only the architects immediately realized that changes were taking place. And so, still today, if we want to understand something about the way the auditorium was transformed as it passed from actors in flesh and blood to simulacra on screen, it is to their rare but not exceptional reflections from the 1910s and '20s that we must turn. As with Kiesler, we are talking about brief texts, where years of professional experience are condensed into a few

pages. Those who take the time to rummage through the by-now
yellowed papers will be repaid with a series of illuminating considerations like this one:

> A movie auditorium should not be built like a playhouse or a concert
> hall; the project that the architect needs to realize is something else
> entirely. The front rows are no longer the best; the side seating
> envisaged by playhouses with circular plans—places from which,
> looking ahead, one sees elegant boxes—are worthless in a movie
> theatre; the auditorium is dark; one looks at the screen and not the
> public.

This peremptory judgment by Robert Mallet-Stevens, chief exponent of
the French modernist school and acclaimed scenographer of about
fifteen silent films, including Marcel l'Herbier's *L'inhumaine*, summarizes the essential aspects of at least a decade of experiments. It would be
difficult to find a better point of departure, but the almost aphoristic
density of passages like this one forces us to proceed step by step.

Mallet-Stevens points first of all to the question of the screen. From
the sixteenth century onward, the introduction of perspectival scenery
had meant that an ideal view could be had from only one position: in
Italian aptly named the *posto del Principe* ("Prince's place," in English,
"King's dais"), it was the seat, usually facing straight ahead in the first
row of the loggia on the theatre's symmetrical axis, where the sovereign perched during a performance and from which the perspective
was drawn. The closer the spectator was to this point, the more
complete was the illusion. With respect to this hierarchical principle,
the movie screen's size had spontaneously introduced a sort of democ-
ratization of the gaze; and though it would continue in live theatres,
the Italian playhouse model, which rigidly separated seating based on
the quality of the view, lost its meaning. At the movies—this was the
first lesson—there were no bad seats, with the partial exception of the
first rows. In the playhouse, these at least had the advantage of being
close to the stage, but at the movies they were less appetizing, crammed
as they were under the screen, and became the reserves for latecomers

and snobs. In the 1950s, the young critics of the *Cahiers du cinéma* adopted the habit of taking these seats so disliked by the "normal" public, as if they were a sort of recognition—a stigmata, even—of the true enthusiast, whose desire to "enter into the film" won out over the objective discomfort of the accommodations.

But this was not all. Little by little, beginning in the seventeenth century, various rows of boxes had sprung up around the orchestra seating. Leaning out from the boxes the spectators were surely less comfortable than they would have been on the main floor, but the auditorium's form (oval, rectangular, bell-shaped) allowed them to keep continuous watch over what happened on stage as well as in front of them, in the boxes across the way occupied by the other women and men anxious as they were to participate in the same social ritual. As we have seen, notwithstanding the repeated protests of the dramatists and actor–managers who would have preferred a more rigorous respect for the Renaissance theorists' prescriptions on the use of lighting to reinforce scenic impact, through most of the nineteenth century the auditorium remained partially illuminated during the show, favoring the public's inclination to take pleasure in seeing and being seen. Only with the invention of electricity, thanks to centralized lighting, would the practice of darkening the auditorium—one of the foundations of the Wagnerian reform, along with the double proscenium arch, the forward-facing fan-shaped seating, and the disappearance of the orchestra pit into the "mystic chasm"—become common, creating a climate of collective concentration and silent expectation, but also making impossible the game of glances that for many, from the beginning, had been one of the principal joys of attending the theatre. It was what Angelo Ingegneri, the man responsible for staging the first modern production of *Oedipus Rex* at the Teatro Olimpico, had asked for ever since 1598:

> It is important for the light to hit the stage, the perspective, and the proscenium but not spill into the house, where the spectators are. The darker the house is, the brighter the scene will seem; conversely, if the house is illuminated, the light will damage the spectators' view, and what should be clearly seen will appear less clear and less desirable.

For this reason, it is advisable to extinguish all the lights that have remained on for the public's convenience at the beginning of the performance.

For about three centuries, only on rare occasions would Ingegneri and the others be satisfied on this specific point. Before the rise of the picture palace, complete darkness in the auditorium had remained an exception, apart from in Italian theatres, where much to the surprise of travelers (who often reported their findings with some wonder), it was more common for the lights to be extinguished when the show began. Now, suddenly, due only to the power of technology, the movie theatre forced its audience to submit to total darkness for the entire film; and so, from that moment on, as Mallet-Stevens had noted, the side boxes no longer made sense, and decorations became useless.

The dismissal—a very partial dismissal, in fact—of the Italian play-house model did not happen all at once. Multifunctional spaces, which could house either a film, play or opera, and were thus designed according to old plans, continued to be built for quite some time. But the citation from Mallet-Stevens tells us that, by 1924, experts shared the idea that cinema had its own specificity and viewing style. Little by little, even the critics lacking any architectural consciousness would note the separation that had taken place. "The conditions of the cinematic specta-tor," Umberto Barbaro wrote in 1936,

> are very different than those of the playgoer: enveloped by darkness, he cannot show himself and his clothing off, nor linger about admiring the rest of the public and its precious elegance: he can't chat with his neighbors without being hushed, and, in a word, can't do anything but stare at the luminous rectangle of the screen; because if he is not allowed to be distracted from this vision, if the film being projected doesn't interest him, all he can do is get up and leave, or abandon himself to sleep, and, in substance, nullify himself as a spectator.

The dark cube essentially remained an Italian playhouse, exactly like those that had been constructed for three and a half centuries; at the same time, however, the total darkness and the size of the screen were a novelty, and ought to be taken as an upgraded realization of the principles inspiring playhouses from Palladio onward: a sort of hyper-theatre gifted with an unprecedented capacity to condition the public.

Neither the architects of the Italian Renaissance nor Wagner could have wished for a more perfect machine. In a hypothetical ranking of aesthetic devices, in fact, the movie theatre would surely take first place for efficacy, with the playhouse at its heels. If the live theatre had secured four (and more rarely, with total darkness, five) of the six elements that characterize cinema's viewing style, in comparison the primitive cinema seems much more distant. As we have seen, the situation could change drastically from venue to venue, and already before the dark cube's triumph, with feature-length films the lengthy process of moving toward the Italian playhouses' spectatorship model had begun. Yet these attempts represent the exception. In the vast majority of cases, before the movie theatre, film projections remained proudly resistant to the rigors of the Vitruvian spectacle: theatre's viewing style was closer to cinema's than were the shows of the early days, when only the collective participation, the large screen size, and partial darkness were truly guaranteed.

Despite this initial struggle, it would be a mistake to minimize the essential fraternity of the viewing styles of the two "auditorium arts," theatre and cinema, at least in their Vitruvian variations. Their kinship becomes increasingly evident if we bear in mind the successive development of moving-image systems and the post-cinematic viewing style that for convenience's sake we may call television, keeping in mind that this is just an approximation, as television is *just one* of the technological supports that promoted the new spectatorship model. Despite the differences, big or small depending on the case, the dark cube remained the winning heresy in the big family of places of performance: a perfect example of innovation within continuity. Nothing even close can be said for television. The lighted lamps, the domestic environment, the abundance of potential distractions (people walking and talking in front of the TV), the small screen size, and private viewing immediately signaled a clean break with the past, even if this upstart's impact on the system of the arts has yet to be fully evaluated.

We must analyze these points one by one. First, there is the novelty
of a cinema that reaches its spectators in their homes. Apart from the
contained costs of the new technology (a precondition of such a capillary
diffusion), nothing a priori required television to become a domestic
medium, as is demonstrated by its initially collective use, when the vast
majority of appliances were found in bars and restaurants and it was
common to get together with friends to watch an evening's programs.
The recent proliferation of television sets in bus and train stations,
airports, and shopping malls (as well as bars and nightclubs) moves in
the exact same direction. It would be difficult, however, to deny that
television has a special vocation of making a place for itself in each family's home, and of dividing the crowd of strangers that once sat in the
dark side by side into a multitude of audiences of one. In some ways, its
ability to privatize the show was a large part of the new technology's
promise and appeal; right from the start, even more than the size of the
screen, the end of the communal regime of viewing seemed the greatest
novelty introduced by TV. The only element that all forms of theatre
and cinema ever had in common was the public of spectators gathered
together in the same place as the performance; it mattered little whether
it was live or filmed. Suddenly, thanks to television, finding oneself
alone, face to face with moving pictures, became a very concrete possibility. And thus watching a film began to resemble a traditionally
individual experience such as silent reading.

Knowing that someone else somewhere else is probably watching the
same show is not enough to cancel out the enormous difference between
these two experiences. It is not so strange, then, that those nostalgic for
the auditorium have insisted on this unprecedented privatization to
defend the ideas that 1) there is an insuperable distance between cinema
at the movie theatre and the fluid world of moving image systems, and 2)
the shadows of the films we got to know on the big screen barely survive
outside of their natural habitat: the picture house. In some cases this
regret for "simultaneous collective reception" led to highly paradoxical
formulations, like Roland Barthes's thesis that a private screening necessarily becomes boring without a true audience, or Susan Sontag's, which
argues that even the most perfect home projection system will fail to

produce the same magic of a movie savored with a "real" public because—as she wrote in one of her most controversial articles on cinema's unrelenting decadence—"since film no longer has a standard size, home screens can be as big as living room or bedroom walls. But you are still in a living room or a bedroom, alone or with familiars. To be kidnapped, you have to be in a movie theatre, seated in the dark among anonymous strangers."

For both Barthes and Sontag, the pleasure of cinema is directly linked to the tension generated by sharing a darkened, circumscribed space with dozens or hundreds of strangers. But Barthes even more explicitly defines this unmistakably sexual excitement, and goes so far as to compare the spectator's receptivity during the film to the sexual availability of the *drague* and of cruising, with an imperceptible (but decisive) slippage from the dark cube to the "dark room" of gay clubs. The desire for strangers would in Barthes's view infuse the images on the screen with a particular energy, which at home (where we are surrounded by all-too-familiar objects lacking any eroticism) disappears completely, to the detriment of the aesthetic experience: "The *eroticization* of the place is foreclosed: television *doomed* us to the family, whose household instrument it has become—what the hearth used to be, flanked by its communal kettle."

Sex has not always achieved such prominence in the cult of the movie theatre; and yet Barthes and Sontag are very important because, with their oh-so-1970s ideology of *jouissance*, they play in an erotic key what is a widespread tune among cinephiles. In the twentieth century, each time their gaze wandered from the screen to the darkness of the house, critics and writers seized upon the image of a clientele that was carefree—in comparison to a bourgeois playhouse audience—rather than one subject to a rigid behavioral code. Instead of an aesthetic device that was different but substantially kindred to the Vitruvian edifice, these critics saw a movie theatre that was notable above all for its spectators—objects of a desire perhaps not carnal, but in any case just as intense as that which Barthes and Sontag describe. Two separate worlds entered into contact, often for the first time. Who were these men and women seated just a few rows away? Where did they come from? In his autobiography, for instance, Sartre recalls how, as a child, the blue-collars, maids, and soldiers encountered at the movie theatre attracted and frightened him at the same time—a feeling of curiosity and instinctive fondness common to many youngsters of his generation. It would be pointless to deny it: in the last century, passion for movies was nourished by this sincere enthusiasm for a humanity that had previously been invisible to the privileged classes, who suddenly found themselves enjoying the same entertainments and the same venues as the untouchables of capitalist society. And for this reason they were driven to celebrate the new art, either for its power to create brotherhood between the classes or for its spontaneously proletarian and revolutionary nature (this depending on the author's political convictions).

Even if we limited ourselves to the first decades of the century, it would not be difficult to find testimonies to this effect: Giovanni Papini, Ricciotto Canudo, Victor Freeburg, Walter Benjamin, Umberto Barbaro, and many others. Compared to the habitués of prose theatres, moviegoers undoubtedly seemed not only uncouth and uneducated, but also extraordinarily real and sincere, not to mention exotic and quaint. The new art for the new classes: an infallible mix for an epoch that had so enthusiastically placed its bets on the nexus of the avant-garde and revolution. Among the first critics, maybe only the Russian formalists, and in particular Boris Eichenbaum, knew to resist this mythology of romantic communion with the nickelodeon masses, and it is probably this anti-bourgeois fascination with a public of "noble savages" that nourished the legend—among many scholars alive today—of the movie theatre as a crossroads of histories and as a privileged place of socialization, where films are only an accessory.

To get back to the spreading of the picture house across Europe and the United States, the first step must be to distinguish accurately the dark cube—understood as an essentially traditional aesthetic device—from those who frequented it and were often completely new to the type of experience that the movie palace offered for the first time to increasingly large proportions of the population: a newfound phenomenon as well, but one that had very little to do with architectural technologies of spectacle, and instead must be tied to the evolution of Western society at the beginning of the twentieth century.

The caesura that was television also takes on new significance when seen from this perspective. If we keep the whole sequence in mind, and therefore stop separating the history of the movie theatre from that of the Italian playhouse, the passage from a cinematic to a post-cinematic viewing style will suddenly be seen in a new light. Rather than the disappearance of the subtle erotic or political complicity induced by the darkness, the decisive element of the rise of the small screen if anything seems to be the refusal of the age-old knowledge that guided the sixteenth-century thespians in their attempts to offer spectators an ever more totalizing aesthetic experience. Perspective, illusionistic scenography (including the prohibition on painting living beings), the strict separation of stage from house, and the artificial darkness, just like the solutions later devised by the dark cube's architects, were introduced with the objective of facilitating the public's reaction: its emotion, its amusement and—why not?—its moral instruction.

Naturally, this required the spectator's cooperation. Still today, to work as it should, the auditorium asks some small sacrifices of its attendees. At the movies or at a play, the public's temporary renouncing of its freedom of speech and movement takes place through a special psychomotor condition. But there is more going on here. Respecting the forced silence and immobility, in fact, the spectator merely repeats the pact made with the filmmaker upon crossing the threshold. Do not resist; let your guard down; give yourself over to the flow of the images. First and foremost in your own interest.

Throughout the central decades of the twentieth century, the film experience was inseparable from this project of disciplining the gaze. In Kafka's words, "the cinema involves putting the eye into uniform, when before it was naked": an image suited as well to the movie camera as to the Vitruvian building with its prohibitions and rituals. Then suddenly, with the advent of television, things began to change. Individual media rejected the notion that it was imperative to submit to a regime of necessity as rigorous as the one that, still today, movie- and playgoers agree to for a couple of hours. At home, on the contrary, there was no longer any reason to do so. Absented from the social ritual, emancipated from a standard code of conduct, television spectators were free, out of the blue, to choose for themselves how to watch the luminous rectangle. Quite simply, with the elimination of group viewing that required everybody not to disturb his neighbor, any sort of behavior in front of the TV became legitimate.

Who could blame us for keeping the lights on or talking over the dialogue, seeking to rid our eyes of the uniform Kafka so criticized? No one, evidently. This is the happily anarchic world we live in: the world of thousands of different devices for image-reproduction, where there is no hierarchy of viewing styles nor any "correct" way of making use of moving-image systems, and so films prosper at once on the big, small, and very small screens. From this point of view, the rise of video is nothing but one of innumerable incarnations of a general crisis of pedagogical institutions (the Family, the School, the University, Criticism . . .).

Naturally, because the conditions in which we watch a film are never irrelevant, each of these experiences will be different from the others. In particular, today it is *communis opinio* that television programs are watched by distracted spectators who accompany their viewing with other activities, or in any case concentrate only partially on the images. In the 1980s, mass media theorists began to describe cinema and television experiences in terms of a radical contraposition between an attentive, concentrated, meditative *gaʒe*, on one hand, and a rapid, wandering, definitively superficial *glance*, on the other. In short, while the dark cube would guarantee a film an involved and receptive audience, domestic viewing would instead mean a reduced participation, bordering on indifference. This representation of the telespectator as a negligent spectator of course does not stand alone; rather, it is accompanied by and partly descends from a series of similar reflections on the ways in which the public's attitude changes at home, due to the primacy of sounds over images or to the substantial homogeneity of the flow that makes it useless even to try to distinguish one program from the next. A constellation of hypotheses about the small screen that makes it the polar opposite of the cinematic cave, with its implicit prison metaphors.

So does the loss of the auditorium's centrality mean the end of traditional attention? Many believe so. And yet, though it is impossible to deny the break between the world of the auditorium and the world of individual media, such readings give us an acute sense of déjà vu. The environment described in most of these studies is a tranquil bourgeois abode, usually occupied by a housewife who leaves the TV on so that the voices keep her company as she does her housework and yet only occasionally raises her eyes toward the screen; but as for the way telespectators are represented, their extreme freedom immediately calls to mind Delluc's beloved *café-chantant* customers and the Benjaminian theory of "reception in a state of distraction" as a peculiarity of cinema and of architecture. And it is in fact "The Work of Art" that allowed Miriam Hansen and other scholars of silent film to posit that the new civilization of moving-image systems rising from the ashes of the twentieth-century auditorium should be greeted as a return to those promising origins after the parenthesis of the dark cube (especially for a female public, finally rescued from patriarchal control). If television is the true medium of "reception in a state of distraction," for Benjamin—who wrote of a cinema that no longer existed in the 1930s but foresaw what some of the elements of the post-cinematic viewing style would be—we could even speak of a *prophetic tardiness*, and welcome individual media as an avant-garde of the masses full of unexplored potential.

Not everyone, truth be told, is so optimistic. Other film historians, like Noël Burch, in fact tend to devalue the glance in favor of the gaze, and are less disposed to admire television viewers' nonchalant behavior toward moving images, films included:

> It is strange to see the many ways in which United States network television constitutes a "return" to the days of the nickelodeon: a continuous showing divided into brief segments of from one to ten minutes, with an audience that drifts in and out as their everyday activities and the control knobs will allow, the incredible mixture of genres, and perhaps especially the confusions between reality and fiction to which television audiences seem so prone.

Burch accuses television of allowing a state "in which pure sensation overwhelms meaning," and argues that it is only a "turning back of the clock, which is anything but innocent," destined to provoke "a sort of bland detachment (clinically observed to be close to a state of narcosis or hypnosis)" through a rejection of the medium's narrative potential in deference to its spectacularity. The same accusations made, once upon a time, against cinema.

As we can see, these positions could not be more distant. The American feminist in love (via Benjamin) with popular culture versus the Franco-American formalist comrade of the European *nouvelle vague*. But rather than rushing to take sides for or against a presumed return to the origins of moving-image systems, perhaps it is more worthwhile to reflect for a moment on the pertinence of such a reading. Do television viewers really closely resemble the first moviegoers? This is the fundamental question. Despite the evident similarities, there are many reasons to resist the temptation to interpret today's condition as a return to the cine-variety. First we have the screen size and the issue of collective viewing; even in strictly Benjaminian terms, if the primitive cinema meant a "collective simultaneous reception" and "reception in a state of distraction," and the movie theatre meant a collective attentive reception (though Benjamin did not make this distinction), the TV spectator would be distinguished by his or her superficial viewing, alone or in the company of a few family members or friends (distraction plus isolation).

And yet the reasons to reject the notion of a circularity of viewing styles are much more profound and far more radical. First of all, as we have ascertained in regard to attempts to create the conditions of an auditorium artificially, the telespectator is not necessarily distracted, and can even follow a movie very closely. As one American scholar wrote, "theorists should not jump to theoretical conclusions just because there is an ironing board in the room" (the very symbol of the inattentive housewife). And today, if we choose to watch a DVD or a program we particularly enjoy, our willingness to become engaged is not much different than it would be at the movies. It is quite possible that, at home on TV, *Vertigo* or *Stromboli* will be less gratifying from a visual point of view, just as in the middle of the 1910s it would have been more complicated to follow Pastrone's *Cabiria* in the back of a poorly ventilated beer hall than it would have been seated in a comfortable chair at Thomas

Lamb's Regent Theatre. More complicated, but not impossible for someone wanting to see those movies.

It is precisely in these ideas—that there is only one legitimate response to a given medium, and each artistic discipline corresponds to one type of spectator—that we see the pernicious influence of Benjamin's essay. Even when they fail to cite it explicitly, theorists of the gaze/glance juxtaposition are simply applying to cinema and television the attentive/distracted coupling that Benjamin used to separate theatre from cinema in "The Work of Art." The concepts remain the same, but what was once called upon to define the advent of twentieth-century modernity (and its culture of shock and superficiality) is now described by a new generation of scholars as the quintessence of a postmodern culture which for them represents the complete negation of the early and mid twentieth century.

Unfortunately, this opinion is quite widespread among today's thinkers, even the greatest. I have in mind Zygmunt Bauman, for example, whose notion of postmodern "fluidity" adapts the categories that Ferdinand Tönnies and Georg Simmel used—one hundred years ago!—to explain the birth of the metropolis and the anomic, individualistic society that had replaced the society of values of the past. In less than fifty years, cinema has shifted from distraction to attention because television came to take its place as the synonym for novelty and popular culture. The thesis that TV represents a return to the cine-variety is highly contestable, but it is easy to understand where it came from. It was established when a generation of silent film scholars raised on Benjamin read their contemporary theorists of mass media, also raised on Benjamin. Thus we have arrived at the simple and fallacious syllogism according to which primitive moviegoers and the television public are the same, or at least increasingly resemble one another, simply because the former was inattentive and the latter also seems inclined to distraction.

Unfortunately, however, this thesis rests on a mistaken premise. Contrary to what Benjamin thought, there is more than one way to appreciate the work of an architect, to go to the theatre, or to look at a painting. If this were not the case, there would be no need for aesthetic devices like the dark cube in the first place, because reception would follow an obligatory path—something that we have seen does not happen (and it is very strange that Benjamin, so ready to note the psychological distinction between the act of reading and the act of transcribing, adopts the opposite approach when he abandons the written word, but this is probably a result of his essentially literary background).

Not all of the first movie spectators watched the images distractedly; nor was every person in the dark cube equally willing to let himself be engaged. A brief Charlie Chaplin comedy captures the attention for a few minutes, and this was perhaps all a crowd of spectators little accustomed to cinema would have been disposed to concede before moving on to the next thing—a new short or a mug of beer—but those brief films required no less attention than does a Mizoguchi or Scorsese film. During a movie, especially if it is long or narratively complex, it is quite easy for spectators to become distracted. And picture houses, in the 1910s as today, worked specifically to prevent anything from pulling the onlookers' attention away from the screen, and to help them fix their attention on a single point, straight ahead, on the oversized cloth facing the seats.

Attention and inattention are at most the (probable) results of a series of different factors, including the material conditions in which spectators attend a film and the viewing style they adopt (itself also a consequence of these conditions). In front of the television, both responses remain possible, just as at the movies—even if the auditorium is conceived purposely to intensify involvement and imposes a series of physical and social constraints to this end, while television on the other hand tends to insert itself more gently into a familiar environment, influencing the public's response in a less blatant (but just as profound!) manner. For this reason, those wishing to classify the various devices designed for image-projection would be better off using more ductile formulae, like the coupling of free/forced. Exploiting this opposition, we can conveniently subdivide the history of moving-image systems into three phases, according to the viewing style that predominates in each:

1) The age of the cine-variety and fairground cinema (from about 1895 to 1915, with after-effects until 1930 and beyond), in which the spectator's attention was required for a limited amount of time and a film

screening was accompanied by other more or less demanding, yet in any case distracting, activities like eating and talking with friends. Partial constraint.

2) The age of the dark cube (from about 1915 to 1975), in which, instead, there took place attempts to launch, along with a new type of film, a rigorous disciplining of viewing practices through architecture and a precise behavioral code. Maximum constraint and, consequently, maximum concentration.

3) The age of individual media (from about 1975 to the present), in which new domestic technologies not only allow but also stimulate the spectator's decreased engagement. Maximum liberty and extremely variable concentration (except, of course, when at the movie theatre, whose rules are still in place).

The decisive point—the one that prevents us from being able to describe the individual media age as a simple return to the conditions of primitive cinema—is the profound difference between the act of *permitting* and the act of *stimulating* the public's decreased participation. One of the most common problems of new media studies is the tendency to describe television in negative terms, for example, as a movie theatre lacking something (the dark, the big screen, the crowd of strangers, the silence): an auditorium where you see the same thing, but not as well and with greater effort because the rules to be followed are less rigid. Such a representation is only partially true, and may at most correspond to the contrast between the gentle anarchy of the cine-variety and the disciplined gaze of the hyper-playhouse that is the dark cube. With television, in fact, not only do the movie theatre's constraints disappear but— thanks to the multiple offerings and the remote control—a series of new elements also condition the spectator's behavior. Following the psychology scholars who separate "involuntary" and "voluntary" attention (as did Hugo Münsterberg in his pioneering treatise on cinema in 1916), we might fruitfully distinguish between involuntary and voluntary inattention and conclude that, whereas the early cinema suffered the public's "reduced" participation (reduced, if nothing else, in terms of time), contemporary individual media deliberately promote a more rhapsodic and superficial engagement. For the same reason, the (absolute) freedom of the telespectator has little in common with the (relative) freedom of the movies' first customers.

As we have seen, this change took at least a generation, counting from the first mass migration of Hollywood films to the American networks. Today TV invites us to dissect the flow of images and let impatience prevail; and yet it was not always this way. Zapping developed as a consequence of the vertiginous growth in the number of programs over a few decades. After an initial phase with few shows (generally speaking up to the end of the 1970s) and a growth phase (the 1980s), we reached a situation of extreme abundance marked by the proliferation of pay and thematic channels (from the mid 1990s) that today offer an unprecedented variety of programming. However, if an unstable gaze is the offspring of our epoch's iconic opulence, such a radical change in the public's habits would have been difficult to achieve without another decisive technological innovation. It was in fact the singular presence of an instrument for orienting ourselves in this chaos— the remote control—that transformed the TV from a home cinema (as the first generation of telespectators experienced it) into an entirely new device. Almost as if it was the possibility of effortlessly jumping from one program to another that gave the small screen its true vocation.

In comparison to the revolution sparked by the remote control, the different (lesser) quality of television's images or sound that has been the object of so much spilled ink, from Marshall McLuhan onward, seems like an insignificant detail. It was only with this revolution, in fact, that the intrinsically anti-Vitruvian and anti-pedagogical viewing style that today distinguishes individual media took shape. Thanks to the remote control, we are catapulted into the realm of absolute freedom, where the absence of external constraints is wedded to the invitation to direct our gaze, attentive or distracted as it may be, onto eternally new objects. Outside of the dark cube, spectators are not necessarily distracted, but filmmakers have to fight moment by moment to capture their attention, in search of contact that is always on the verge of interruption. While at the theatre or movies the public voluntarily subjects itself to a regime of necessity, at home the remote control allows us to move while remaining immobile—in other words, it enables (and encourages) us to seek quicker satisfaction elsewhere, surrendering instantaneously to boredom or curiosity. All we need to do is push a button and the scene before our eyes will radically transform itself, because the auditorium's forced immobility has been replaced by a particularly inebriating simulation of movement that puts us at the center of a universe of sounds and colors ready to change at our pleasure. We need not even get up: planted in our comfortable chair (but always free to say, "enough"), it is the world that changes as we wish it to, taking us from one stage to another, near and far at the same time, with a simple push of a button.

Consequently, today, it is not the presumed return to the heroic age of the silver nitrate pioneers that we must reckon with, but this new condition: the spectator's *extreme volatility*. The changes in cinematic style over the last thirty years, which are the topic of the next chapter, will offer further confirmation of this.

5

The Aesthetic of the Shark

Pornographic and cinematographic images act like those stimuli which produce a reflex action of the nerves through channels which are independent of aesthetic perception.

James Joyce, *The Trieste Notebook* (1909)

Clearly a great classic film will be bad on a small screen, because television is an enemy to the values of classic film, but not to film itself.

Orson Welles

In the brief history of moving-image systems, the movie theatre's absolutism was only a parenthesis. In retrospect, the season of the picture house—of Claudia Cardinale and Marcello Mastroianni projected in panoramic format on the big screen—will be considered a rather circumscribed episode, a brief encounter that today we are all the more inclined to remember nostalgically for its transience, and because just a few years later it seems so distant in time. Fifty years, more or less. Throughout the twentieth century's middle decades, when spectators desperately sought to re-create the movie theatre's artificial darkness and isolation at home, the cinematic viewing style was a hegemonic *forma mentis*. Where the center of the system lay was clear to everyone. For twenty or thirty years, television, the new arrival, had tried to imitate cinema in its style, in its content, but above all in its mode of reception, trusting that it is always possible to use an aesthetic device against its implicit rules and that in this moving-image systems are no exception. Nothing more ordinary. The first telespectators did it when they tried to transform their living room into a mini movie theatre, just like those who, in the dark cube's golden age, entered the auditorium after the film had begun and left before it was finished, or commented aloud on each scene, disturbing their neighbors or perhaps provoking their hilarity with a salacious wisecrack.

Although we encounter a dominant viewing style in each epoch, spectatorship models tend to be conservative, persisting at length even when the conditions that made them possible have disappeared. In all likelihood, even in the future the small screen will remain for many an instrument for watching a bit tardily the new releases of a few years before, *almost* like being at the movies. But, at the same time, thanks to the remote control and video player, television has evolved in a different direction; if the desire to create a semi-theatrical space remains perfectly legitimate, this possibility is only partial, and revocable with the simple push of a button.

Centrality, we should note, does not mean absolute monopoly. Viewing styles are never completely overcome, but live alongside one another, and at most lose the supremacy they enjoyed in a particular historical moment. Considering the long term (from the sixteenth to twentieth centuries), we get the impression that we are witnessing a single cycle that rewards now the disciplining force of architecture, now spectacle's ability to colonize the spaces of everyday life. In the end, just as the movie theatre derives from the Renaissance play-house, so might medieval performance practices be thought of as the ancestors of that world of the fair where the Lumières's and Méliès's films were able to prosper in the first fifteen or twenty years of cinema's life. It is also for this reason that the Vitruvian spectator is not destined to disappear in the presence of individual media. Rather, all signs indicate that the principal characteristic of our time is the end of an absolute hierarchy in viewing styles, so that the picture house no longer occupies the system's vertex but still maintains, if nothing else, a chronological pre-eminence in the circulation of new movies. From this point of view, those nostalgic for the dark cube can sleep soundly: no one considers giving up the movie theatre, because the launching of a film there prepares its successive life on other technical supports and allows for the rapid recovery of a large part of the initial investment, often already in the first weekend of programming.

The change in power relations by now seems a given. Fifty years after the deal between the Hollywood majors and the main American networks, the home screen has become the most capillary method of disseminating moving images. The statistics in this case are to be taken quite seriously. For most of the Western population, watching TV— not just movies but also documentaries, game shows, the news, and sports—today constitutes the chief recreational activity, not to mention the third-placed daily activity in absolute terms, after work and sleep. It would be odd for us to think that this reallocation of leisure does not have a precise influence on the public's attitude toward moving images and aesthetic experience in general. Once, television was colonized by the cinematic viewing style; for the last few years, conversely, the relationship seems inverted: the cinematic is the exception, while television has become the standard referent against which all competition must define itself. And this for the simple reason that— quantitatively—the small screen is now the principal vehicle for moving images in our lives.

We still go to the movies, and in all probability will continue to do so for quite some time. And yet, in the darkness of the cube, spectators increasingly often seek images that resemble those they are used to seeing at home. At least in this sense the auditorium epoch is over, or undergoing extinction. The great transition from the cinematic to the post-cinematic viewing style (television or otherwise) can call itself accomplished, but only now can we intuit what the consequences will be for moving-image systems. TV's influence on cinema dates back at least to the 1980s, and not only because producers learned that a movie theatre release guarantees only a small portion of a single film's future earnings—between broadcast rights, video sales and rentals, and computer games and merchandising. Demand conditions supply, as Hollywood specialists know: movies change first of all because spectators change; and spectators are now decreasingly attracted by classical cinema's conventions. Impelled by this pressure, filmmakers (also recruited in growing numbers from the new generations whose tastes were formed in front of the small screen) have begun giving space in their films to a television aesthetic.

A post-auditorium cinema does not yet exist. We still cannot say anything very precise about the tremendous upheaval that is really just beginning, and yet the contradictory nature of contemporary experiments begins to expose its most marked characteristics. Television forces directors to respond to the freedom of a spectator who is always encouraged to take a peek at other channels. In the remote-control epoch, each movie fights to win the public's attention, and it is precisely with this prospect of competition that many films are conceived from the very start.

The spectator's volatility has changed everything. The movie theatre epoch was poor and starved of images (though extraordinarily richer than the pre-photographic age), whereas the world we live in is characterized by an unprecedented crowding. For every frame we give our attention to, there are many thousands that pass by unobserved, preemptively thwarting the grand dreams of the cinephiles of the 1960s: to be able one day to say they had seen every—and they mean every—film. Such a desire, regardless of what we think of it, today cannot even be imagined. In this new situation of a merciless fight for survival, the filmmaker knows in advance that he or she will have to conquer the public's assent moment by moment. Slacken the tension for an instant, and the viewer will change the channel, promptly registered by a Set Meter that gauges approval every thirty or sixty seconds—at such tight intervals that no decline in interest will go unobserved.

The twentieth-century cinema knew how to take advantage of the semi-theatrical conditions that the auditorium lent to movies. As long as it was necessary to leave the house, buy a ticket, and enter a crowded venue, the institution worked for directors, ensuring them two hours of stable attendance and, ideally, continuous attention. Television is not capable of doing this, nor does it propose to. Outside of the dark cube, a filmmaker must never slow things down, unless he wants to lose the zapping spectator caught up in the vortex of channel surfing, sucked in by the gravitational pull of competing programs. The European and American *nouvelle vague* experiments in the 1960s, in contrast, were made possible in part by the constraints of architecture and social ritual; but the same is true for classic Hollywood films, with their alternation between fullness and void, between major and minor scenes. The dark cube's crisis put an end to this privileged condition, and obliged cinema to compromise with the elementary—and for this all the more powerful—logic of advertising. Consensus, in television, is gained frame by frame because the battle never relents: frame by frame, and by any means. When the competition is so stiff, the tools for holding the viewer's attention are quite limited in number, and relying on those visual and auditory stimuli to which humans respond in predictable ways may be one of the surest strategies of achieving the objective.

The point is obviously crucial. Television producers appeal to this very principle when they argue that some images have the power of seduction and others send viewers running—that, for example, the voices of two people arguing push ratings instantly skyward, while a close-up of an eye has just the opposite effect. Is this true? Such experience-based theories seem about as reliable as an urban myth, but over the years more serious investigations have been conducted. In fact, since psychologists and anthropologists began to work with the big multinationals' copywriters in postwar America, inaugurating the epoch of hidden persuaders, no research in this direction has been neglected: the general public's likes and dislikes, desires and intolerances, have found hordes of diligent social scientists ready to catalog them in minute detail according to race, gender, and geographical location, as well as age, earning, and education range. Many of these reactions depend on cultural imprinting, but studies have shown that some responses transcend the confines of this or that community and are instead inscribed in the genetic code of *Homo sapiens sapiens*. Fairly early (at the beginning of the 1960s) scientists discovered, for example, that the male subject's pupil automatically dilates when it sees a photograph of a shark or of a naked woman (a clear sign of interest), whereas a photo of a baby or a naked man produces the same reaction in females. More recent studies confirm that the brain tends to react instinctively to photographs as if it were in the presence of what they represent. The spectator knows that the tiger on the screen is not there in front of him, but this knowledge does not influence his immediate response because the human visual apparatus is not programed to distinguish between a thing and its representation, and so sends the brain the same signals it would if it were facing a real predator. The distinction between the real tiger and the image of it happens only in a second moment, thanks to experience and rational analytical faculties that reassure us of the non-danger of the images before our eyes. It is in virtue of this awareness that we cannot speak of "illusion" in the fullest sense for cinema (spectators, unlike Plato's prisoners, know they are seeing a show), and if we really do not want to relinquish the term, we must adopt it only in a diluted sense. To explain people's attitudes in the presence of moving frames, a sort of theory of "double truth" seems necessary—one that at the same time recognizes both the eye's inability to separate the original from its reproduction and the constant awareness that we are in any case dealing with a fiction: yes, I see a hungry tiger standing before me; no, that tiger does not pose a threat to me.

The power of these elementary stimuli (not all images have the same force, obviously) lies in the fact that we cannot stop this instinctive response even if we want to. Attraction, repulsion, desire: we are genetically programmed to react that way. And thus it is not difficult to understand why copywriters have employed innumerable methods of exploiting these instincts in promotion of their product. Television began to systematically adopt this advertising logic later, probably around the 1980s, and now even cinema seems to be taking the same road. Things changed quite a bit when films began to be conceived, from the very start, for their first TV appearance. In front of the small screen, the curiosity to discover what is on the other channels lies in constant ambush, and competition based on just a few seconds redefines the rules of the game. Forced to obtain approval for every blink of the eye, a director must take the *primacy of the represented over the representation* very seriously, so that he risks turning into a fairground barker, flattening his style into that of advertising. It is in fact likely that a considerable part of contemporary cinema's uncertainty is due to this need to compromise with the individual media's viewing style without completely betraying its own history.

The confrontation cannot be postponed. Obviously, negating the film's new conditions certainly will not solve the problem. The first step is to articulate the reasons that the new situation unsettles film theorists, accepting as a given the inherent tension between the desire to view certain images and the aesthetic experience to which such visions are only sometimes connected. Banalizing a bit: the opening scene of *Le Mépris*, where Brigitte Bardot is completely naked, has an obvious appeal for any heterosexual adult male, independent of his broader interest in Godard's filmography. The twentieth century's auteurs were for quite some time too wrapped up in the battle to see cinema recognized as a respectable art form to bother with this problem. The leading man's charm? The starlet's eroticism? Little more than a duty to pay for realizing one's film. But then television came along and—through that form of mass plebiscite that is the remote control—rendered immediately evident the instinctive and pre-rational nature of our response to visual images (Godard's genius was in knowing that actors' bodies could become pop objects, just as on the canvases of American art of the day: Brigitte Bardot who does Brigitte Bardot, in the manner of Andy Warhol's Marilyn who does Marilyn).

Aside from Thomas Edison, widely derided for believing that cinema would remain "an invention that could do for the eye what the phonograph could do for the ear," we had to wait for the 1980s and Serge Daney to find a critic who drew attention to this constant predominance in film history of the *what* over the *how*. It is not strange that it was a cinephile turned TV and mass-media critic who found it was necessary to rethink the peculiar characteristics of people's passion for moving pictures. Daney's fundamental idea—as always, in his case, disseminated in dozens of occasional writings—is that four-fifths of cinema was simply recordings of the live or ad hoc spectacles that the public wanted to see at any cost, even from a distance, as long as the image was clear: something like Brigitte Bardot naked, to pick up the earlier example. Art, when we can really call it art, would be an exception or a sort of side dish, to such an extent that the film historian might be tempted to speak of it only in the rare cases when the director used the movie camera as something more than a simple recording technology.

If in the 1950s Bazin's question had been "What is cinema?," Daney's, who, significantly, lived at a time marked by the indiscriminate proliferation of moving pictures, might be "When is cinema art?" It comes as no surprise, then, that one of his last projects before he died in 1993 at forty-eight years of age was to make a list of the things that "people wanted to see independent of mediation": that is to say, a cinema devoid of any aesthetic concerns. Daney only had time to draft this list, largely built on concrete cases and on the very first films, when cinema's servile attitude was more explicit and there was no need to feign or seek pretexts justifying the medium's attachment to reality. The Passion of Christ, kings and queens, exotic landscapes, strongmen, fairs, magic acts, freaks—in all cases, "films without a story," where the movie camera's only job was to bring the spectator nearer to the coveted object of desire.

Of course, precisely because it was provisional and partial, Daney's list would need to be rounded out, perhaps by flipping through production houses' early catalogs, where all the genres of "cinematic views" are itemized: public executions, dazzling displays, and anything extravagant—great natural disasters (the Kantian sublime?), circus acrobatics, explicit sexual acts. In an delightful representation of his life's work, Georges Méliès wrote in 1907:

> The varieties within this category are innumerable; it includes comic skits, comic operas, burlesques and comedies, peasant stories, the so-called chase scenes, clown acts, acrobatic acts, graceful, artistic, or exotic dance turns, ballets, operas, stage plays, religious scenes, scabrous subjects, plastic tableaux, war scenes, newsreels, reproductions of news items, accident reports, catastrophes, crimes, assassinations, etc.—many more than I can list—as well as the most sober tragedies. The cinematic realm knows no bounds.

Even later, though, according to Daney, the situation would not change much. Twentieth-century cinema for the most part limited itself to offering a comfortable view of the shows that would have been too dangerous or even just too expensive to attend live, allowing anyone who paid to enter and feel as if he were participating in an event that previously had been difficult to observe in everyday life, whether it be a Bengal tiger hunt or Catherine Deneuve revealing her perfect breasts. From this point of view, the opening scene of *Citizen Kane*, where the camera overtakes the gate of Kane's estate with the "No trespassing" sign, could be interpreted as a heraldic emblem of cinema itself: the technology that breaks down barriers and enables us to bring into the light that which before had remained in the dark.

Perhaps Daney's thesis should be reformulated in the following terms: in the twentieth century we had two different histories of cinema—the history of cinema as the history of a particular medium, and the history of cinema as the history of the art of film. In itself, this affirmation should not be all that surprising. Does not the same thing happen with writing? How many of the words we write are born from an impulse that we would define as "artistic"? Even in epochs with a scarcity of paper and parchment (and hence more attentive to leaving behind only what was important), we are speaking of a laughably low percentage. Movies are therefore no exception. And yet, despite the fact that all the amateur documentaries and videos ought to put us on alert against a facile assimilation, criticism confused these two very different histories for quite some time. Finally, a handful of years ago, television revealed that moving images are not always art, and, indeed, they almost never are, showing at the same time the extent to which the primary desire to see had a decisive role in people's passion for cinema.

This disorientation was also made possible because cinema willingly served that originary drive, offering itself at one and the same time as the art of the film and as a recording technology. The equivocation lasted until recently. Before the advent of television there were no other ways to watch moving pictures; in the world of internet and videophones this confusion, conversely, would no longer be possible. And yet, precisely because cinema has availed itself of this ambiguous condition for so long, it would be a mistake to insist too much on its radical difference from the small screen. The contrast, in other words, was never sharp. Even the 20 percent of films designed to be art made recourse to the same enticements to rouse the spectator's curiosity, take him to the movie theatre, and keep him chained in the darkness of the auditorium. Cinema's victory over theatre depended in part on its superior ability to satisfy the elementary visual drive: more gorgeous actors, more spectacular special effects, more splendiferous decorations, more fascinating settings. Everything—a not irrelevant detail—at a lower price.

Gramsci had noted this back in 1916:

> The reason for the success of the cinema and its absorption of former theatre audiences is purely economic. The cinema offers exactly the same sensations of the popular theatre, but under better conditions, without the choreographic contrivances of a false intellectualism, without promising too much while delivering little. The usual stage presentations are nothing but cinema . . . The cinema, which can fulfill this function more easily and more cheaply, is more successful than the theatre and is tending to replace it.

The role of luxury and abundance in classic Hollywood cinema is well documented by the protagonists of that epoch: when directors of the 1930s and '40s did not know exactly where to put camera, they always chose a wide-angle shot to capture the entire set, for such grandeur would always impress the public. But, more than anything else, it was the actors and actresses who counted: Greta and Alida, Clark and Gary, Mirna and Audrey, with their erotic charge vaunted and irresistible, or instead veiled and more subtle.

All of these things were part of the rules of the game. As a popular art, finally capable of satisfying the basic need to see, cinema could not do without them. For the entire twentieth century, the sexual allure of actors' bodies was one of the motors powering the cinephiliac passions of critics and simple enthusiasts; and if we re-read the journal articles of the golden age, we cannot help but be struck by the numerous declarations of love for the diva of the day that sprout right up in the middle of a most serious (or earnest) review. In the 1950s, in particular, the young François Truffaut filled the pages of *Cahiers du cinéma* with lists like this one, published under the entry "fetishism" in a very articulate *Cinépsicopathia-sexualis* in a special issue, "Love of cinema," from December 1954:

> Jane Russell's, Gina Lollobrigida's, Martine Carol's chests; Marilyn Monroe's, Mae West's, Lana Turner's backsides; Marlene Dietrich's, Betty Grable's legs; Lauren Bacall's, Gail Russell's, May Britt's eyes; Simone Simon's, Joan Greenwood's, June Allyson's, Claire Guibert's voices; Katherine Hepburn's freckles; Gloria Grahame's lisp; Clara Calamai's torn skirt in *Ossessione*; Alice Fay's stockings in *Old Chicago*, Elina Labourdette's brassiere in *Les dames du bois de Boulogne*, and all of the slit skirts, pleated and tight, seen in American movies.

Needless to say, as a director Truffaut, unlike Godard, believed whole-heartedly in his actresses.

In the same moment that cinephiles willingly crossed the line between love for movies and love for the women they saw in the movies, however, a conflicting tendency persisted. No one had ever spoken in these terms of Madame Bovary or Lucia Mondella, nor would they do so later; as long as films wanted to be appreciated as works of art, cinema's dual nature could become truly embarrassing. We have already encountered the avant-garde directors of the 1920s and their obsession with purity, and it should not surprise us that articles like Truffaut's were greeted with suspicion by his comrades, worried that cinema would devolve into the burlesque that it had been so difficult to gain distance from.

In this attempt to separate the art of the film from the technology of image-reproduction, though, the auditorium did its work tremendously well. Thanks to the dark cube, the cineastes of the epoch prior to the remote control could measure out the ingredients, soliciting the specta-tor's primary visual drive without catering completely to it. They played with the confusion of levels, and this was their strength. In the twentieth century, perhaps no one knew how to reconcile the demands of great art and market better than filmmakers, doomed—far more than those who expressed themselves in music, painting, or literature—to seek a mini-mum financial success by the implacable laws of competition and profit.

During a century in which the greatest writers and painters often refused communication with the public, cinema was so important to the system of the arts precisely because of its ability and its need never to completely forsake a relationship with spectators. But since the paying public would not leave the auditorium until the projection was over, just like Sophocles and Shakespeare in their time, directors could hold on to some of their cards for later; that is, they could make use of that elementary desire to see *more*, the better to engross the spectator in the story.

If what I have said until now about the auditorium's disciplining power is true, Daney's judgment could even be turned on its head. *Only* 20 percent of cinema was art? Or instead, and more accurately, *as much as* 20 percent? In short, we ought to ask whether, without the dark cube and its particular viewing style, the percentage of films devoid of any artistic objective would not actually have been much higher: not four-fifths but nine-tenths, or maybe no less than 99 percent of the total. Which is exactly what happened with television, whose (presumed) passion for live broadcast might in fact be the best proof that the recording technology definitely got the better of art, after the fragile compromise that lasted for most of the twentieth century.

Outside of the dark cube, where everything is faster, the basic desire to see gained the upper hand once again. In fact, perhaps the true similarity of the original cinema and contemporary moving images is that, in both cases, a very small portion of pictures are filmed with any artistic intent whatsoever. Edison's prediction, for instance, today seems reductive, but less in error than it would have thirty or forty years ago. And on the small screen—we know it all too well—everything is riding on just a few seconds: an obnoxious line, an unpleasant situation, an unattractive presenter will compel the person on the other side of the box to push the fatal button and seek to satisfy his voracity for images and stories elsewhere.

Instinctive reactions are ruthless. Because the yardstick of approval and disapproval has changed, the battle is now fought ecstasy by ecstasy. Given the public's permanent volatility, it is not difficult to understand why directors are practically obligated to turn to basic impulses like attraction, disgust, fear. If they do not manage to dilate the spectators' pupils, they will lose them forever. The small screen, in this sense, is wholly Pavlovian: it draws on these stratagems perforce, appealing to the public with new bids and endless *coups de théâtre*. And so contemporary film-makers rely above all on the shark, on the baby, and on the pin-up girl—according to the principle of the internet publicity banner from which half-naked girls look at us with bedroom eyes, inviting us to click.

Nothing better reveals moving images' ever-increasing iconic atom-ism than the difference between the stage or film actress and the top model (in extreme cases, the porn star), between the woman who *has* a body and the woman who *is* a body. In recent years, though, even cinema has come up against this new situation. No longer aided by the audito-rium, directors have to invent new tools to capture a viewer who is increasingly in search of instant gratification, even when he or she is at the movies, where spectators now expect the same visual stimuli offered by television.

With the increased permeability of the big and small screens (as well as their commercial integration), New Hollywood's big stylistic trends can all be interpreted as responses to the end of the dark cube's central-ity. For at least thirty years, movies' costs have been greatly affected by the growing need to produce amphibious works, readily able to make headway in and out of the picture house. Among scholars today, there seems to be consensus on the matter. The critics who study New Hollywood's style in fact generally agree that the films produced in the last thirty years still follow the principles of classical cinema, but none-theless indicate a general transformation in filmmakers' modes of expression. The major changes from the late 1970s onward could be summarized in a handful of points (the tendency to film directly in digital format, which will quite possibly catch on in coming years, for now only relates to a very small portion of Hollywood's production, and to only one key director, Michael Mann, who uses it to achieve a very warm, spectacular nighttime photography). They are:

1) Increasingly rapid editing. Between 1930 and 1960 the average shot ranged from seven to eleven seconds, but at the beginning of the new millennium this length was reduced to less than half that: between

three and six seconds, depending on genre. And not just in action scenes, for this rhythm is often found in the most common shot/reverse-shot dialogue scenes as well. Only in truly exceptional cases does this acceleration render a scene difficult to follow or even incomprehensible; almost always, in fact, the sequences with this syncopated editing remain spatially coherent. It is pointless to note that this type of editing tends to be much more elliptical than the standards of classic cinema.

2) The recourse to zoom lenses, increasingly widespread since the 1970s, despite or perhaps because of their slightly distorting effect, whereas classical Hollywood cinema traditionally opted for short focal lengths. The new system allows directors to shoot from afar, using more than one camera, with notable savings of time (and money). From a stylistic point of view, we owe to zoom lenses the prevalence of "rack-focus" (the changing of focus within the same frame so as to make a character or detail that was previously in the background emerge). This is quite the opposite of the tendency, just after the Second World War, to film scenes with great depth of field, letting spectators choose where to direct their attention in each frame.

3) The close position of the camera during dialogue. If classical cinema was a cinema of bodies, the New Hollywood cinema is one of faces. This has reduced the expressive resources at actors' disposal, as it forces them to use a more private and intimate acting style, independent of their personal talents or inclinations. If James Stewart was famous for his hand gestures in particularly intense dramatic moments and Cary Grant had developed a preference for strange poses and oblique lines, today it would be quite difficult for an actor to play similarly in front of the camera, except of course in action scenes, where the range of solutions is at any rate quite limited. Now, mouths, eyes, and eyebrows are the main and almost only source of information (and emotion) for the public: actors' bodies have lost a large part of their ability to communicate to spectators anything besides their obvious physical appeal.

4) The camera's extreme mobility. If the great twentieth-century auteurs were often true masters of the long take, and best displayed their

virtuosity by tailing their actors, today important films in which the director fails to show off with complicated movements—even if only accompanying a banal conversation while characters pass from one room to another—are hard to come by. The growing use of these solutions was made possible by new lighter and more stable cameras like the Steadicam, but this increased freedom of action completely transformed the sense of traditional stylistic choices like tracking, pan, and crane shots. That which once served to highlight an important node of the story today has simply become a means of visually enhancing a scene. So, from the mid 1990s, the most common way of filming a group of people seated around a table, or someone who speaks in a phone booth, is to circle dizzily around them. For the vast majority of the last generation's Hollywood filmmakers, the camera's constant mobility has now become the necessary precondition for any particularly lengthy shot. Something similar also happened with music videos, where, after the syncopated editing of the 1980s, in the next decade— beginning at least with Massive Attack's *Unfinished Sympathy*—the sequence shot established itself for five or six seasons as the most typical way to introduce the new success of a rock band.

5) The increased use of digital technologies, which brings cinema ever closer to that aesthetic of total image control, and which was until recently the prerogative of painting. If in the beginning the recourse to computer graphics was mainly limited to a few genres (horror, science fiction, fantasy, war), or anyway to just those films in which postproduction served to create immediately evident special effects, at the turn of the millennium a new phase began. With the dissemination of the necessary software, computer mediation has been used ever more often to add very minimal touches, with decidedly realistic intent—for example, to eliminate a bothersome reflection on a window, to change the shade of a dress, or to age an actor imperceptibly. *O Brother, Where Art Thou?*, from 2000, in this sense represents a real watershed because it was the first feature-length film subject *in its entirety* to digital color correction. The Coen brothers had planned to shoot the film in Texas during the summer, but had to move to Mississippi, where the light was completely different and the

landscape was not arid and dusty enough, forcing them to recolor every frame artificially—a practice that has since become increasingly common.

6) Finally, the transformation of screenplays. Classical cinema was built upon the gradual development of the story, which "grew" slowly but inexorably toward a narrative and spectacular climax: a series of increasingly engaging scenes up until the decisive confrontation and dénouement. The new blockbusters tend instead to be organized around a radically different compositional strategy, stringing together a large number of sequences with strong visual impact but weak connections to one another, like a rollercoaster. In the most extreme cases, the story becomes a pretext for a chain of shots able to keep the spectator pinned to the seat—even at the cost of transforming the story into little more than a veneer of continuity for the movie's single dramatic moments; a little bit like the musicals of yesteryear, perhaps not by chance recently back in style.

In all six cases, the phenomenon neither describes just Hollywood films nor only those shot in the United States, but is, rather, a general trend in contemporary cinema. To explain this profound transformation, critics have considered a number of possible causes, from the prestige of stylistic solutions introduced by innovators like Orson Welles or Alfred Hitchcock, to the change in production habits (such as the penchant for filming with more than one camera, which multiplies the quantity of the shots, and thus the editor's possibilities), to strictly technological improvements (such as digital editing, which makes it much easier to intervene frame by frame). Each of these elements surely was and continues to be significant; and yet there is a certain consensus among scholars that television's influence is a key factor in the change. Without downplaying technology's role here too (actors' auditions are recorded on film; the Steadicam's viewer is a video monitor; computer editing means that the film takes its definitive shape on the small screen, and so on), directors' awareness that their films have to work even once the run in the theatres comes to an end leads them to adopt a style that—precisely because of its intensity—seems particularly suited to home consumption.

There is no reason to contest this interpretation. Cinematic innovations in the age of individual media are all well explained by the need to imagine movies, from the start, in terms of the moment when they will leave behind film and silver nitrate and be deposited onto that which—as things now stand—is the most stable support: the video disc. Exactly as had happened with the dark cube, the victory of a new spectatorship model triggered the transformation of movies' style. Television's influence probably appears most blatantly in the predominance of the close-up and the extreme close-up (especially in dialogue scenes) as a direct consequence of the reduced screen size and of the need to assure the legibility of actors' features on domestic video (item 3, above). The diffusion of rapid editing, of rack-focus, and of fast camera movements (items 1, 2, and 4) can by other paths be easily traced back to the new viewing style. Without the movie theatre as intensifier of the aesthetic experience, sudden changes of plane and of framing would produce a series of small shocks designed to hold the public's attention, and thus forestall the dreaded zapping. A similar discourse is valid, moreover, for the process of digitally altering the single frame, the multiplication of recording supports, and the use of filters (item 5). Saturated images in fact also help to maximize the impact on the spectator, making every shot particularly attractive with special effects and computer graphics: not necessarily "beautiful" in the traditional sense, but capable of sparking interest at first sight. In these cases a falsely dirty photography can serve the same end as well as a colored filter, exactly as the abrupt movement from one recording support to another (video, 35mm, 16mm, Super 8, and so on) produces the same result—a sure antidote against the public's fickle nature. In the end, this imperative directly influences the construction of the story, too, if screenplays structured by high-impact micro-segments (item 6) can be interpreted as an umpteenth response to television spectators' inconstancy, because they never let the tension fall below a certain level and make even a partial viewing of a movie gratifying.

Somehow, then, all these points converge. As David Bordwell wrote, in contemporary cinema, "even ordinary scenes are heightened to compel attention and to sharpen emotional resonance." But this, I should specify right off the bat, happens strictly because the shifting of the movie theatre toward the periphery of the moving-image system has created an increasingly intolerant spectator—that is to say, a spectator much more inclined to judge the product fragment by fragment and to expect the most from each one. If the smallest stylistic unit of twentieth-century cinema was the shot as a block of space–time, in the last quarter of the century this tended increasingly to coincide with a single frame (until digital cameras make even this parameter obsolete).

Exactly like the extensive recourse to basic visual drives (Brigitte Bardot or the shark), the general stylistic accentuation of contemporary cinema can be read as a direct consequence of the new post-Vitruvian viewing style. The proliferation of competing claims on the attention of spectators, indispensable to the small screen, requires directors constantly to offer new stimuli, again and again: colors, shapes, rhythms, contrasts, dissonance, and so on. Those who pay the price first are those who do not adapt to the new standards, which may remind us of the first cinephiles' irritation at theatre's (slow) speed, as Jean Epstein relates in a 1921 essay, where he is forced to admit that "the habit of strong sensations, which cinema above all is capable of producing, blunts theatrical sensations, which are, moreover, of a lesser order." The same judgment that was also made by one of the major avant-garde directors of the first part of the century, the Italian Anton Giulio Bragaglia:

Anyone who goes to the movies cannot rehabituate himself to theatre. If cinema goes 300 kilometers per hour, theatre goes 30. The audience has gotten used to the picture show's great sensations and can no longer be satisfied by those of theatre. The public is a telephone fine-tuned to hear great intuitions, while theatre is still a primitive old microphone. How can you go by stagecoach in the epoch of the airplane?

Once the average pacing is raised, in other words, anyone who continues to go forward at the former cruise speed will be immediately disadvantaged. It is just that now, for the first time, cinema finds itself in the position of being the one that has to run to keep up.

In general, remakes of the great classics of the 1940s and '50s best verify the inherent dangers in this ideology of absolute presence and visibility; take, for instance, Paul Schrader's (bad) movie *Cat People* (1982), with its metamorphosis of the woman-panther shot in broad daylight instead of the (truly terrifying!) shadow effects conceived by Jacques Tourneur in the original from 1942. Now that filmmakers must constantly surprise the spectator, allusion or even just postponement has become increasingly difficult. Today this obligation affects every aspect of a movie, from the framing of individual shots to the construction of the story. The need to say and show everything means, for example, the disappearance of playing with the off-screen, which had such an important place in the history of the seventh art (so much so that Gilles Deleuze saw in it one of cinema's own "philosophical concepts"). Manipulating time, which after the Second World War had became one of the key areas of experimentation, now also becomes impossible. However, as I have mentioned, it is not only modernist cinema that finds itself unarmed outside the dark cube, because the entire dialectic of fullness and void characteristic of Hollywood classicism suffers the effects of this new situation, where fullness is always awarded to the detriment of the sparseness constituting its natural correlative (if nothing else because it allows abundance to stand out by contrast).

The ubiquity of moving images, for which now the movie theatre is only the first step on a much longer journey destined to end elsewhere, dooms to the margins any film that too insistently follows the classical paths. What about Robert Bresson's and Ernst Lubitsch's off-screens, or Yasujiro Ozu's and Michelangelo Antonioni's representations of pure temporality? The new cinema needs to saturate the image and to surprise the public far more than it needs to induce them to reflect on Kantian transcendentals. But this is not negative per se, and when we speak of this poetics of opulence we must not forget that the extreme attention to detail it requires potentially represents a value—with the paradox, perhaps, that we have never been so close to the *caméra-stylo* dreamed up in the 1940s by Alexandre Astruc as when computer graphics are accessible to everyone.

Unfortunately, in the vast majority of cases, the principal effect of this catering to the spectator by technological means has meant a growing stylistic trivialization. A look back in time, however, might persuade us to be less pessimistic. Unlike the other arts, cinema pays the price of instability, determined by technology's incessant progress. In the last century, no painter or novelist had to deal with an earthquake of a magnitude equal to that produced by the rise of sound, color, or panoramic format. Never. Cinema's strength (but also its weakness) is historically tied to the provisional character of the tools available to the director. Every time a generation of filmmakers learned to use the technology on hand with some proficiency, a radical renewal of those tools swooped down and carried away the confidence they had finally gained. It took almost ten years to learn how to use sound, and a bit longer (but with less damage) to use color, while many never learned to master Cinemascope at all. And the zoom? Its indiscriminate use disfigures many of the movies shot in the 1970s, even those by indisputable masters like Roberto Rossellini, Joseph Losey, Robert Altman, or Billy Wilder. Similarly, though in *The Shining* Stanley Kubrick found the perfect use for the Steadicam, in the majority of cases the tracking shot's emancipation from the tracks coincided with the triumph of movement for movement's sake and a lack of interest in stylizing space. And now come the computer, mass special effects, and soon the disappearance of film . . .

Directors are still condemned to reinvent themselves every ten years. Yet we might think that the net result of all these innovations is largely positive, for twentieth-century cinema was so rich partly thanks to the perpetual precariousness that, routing generations of masters, obligated the few survivors to keep on experimenting. All things considered, the myth of the periodic beheading of the king, which through James George Frazer's *Golden Bough* inspired Francis Ford Coppola's finale in *Apocalypse Now*, is not a bad paradigm for describing the waste of talent that has marked the art of the film.

The changes in the recording apparatus are not the only factor in this very rapid turnover, and so—regardless of individual directors' ability to find financing for their new projects—the great filmmakers' creative periods seem incomparably contracted in comparison to those of their writer and artist counterparts. Something similar can be said, in fact, of viewing styles. To an extent, we have already seen it. Having entered the picture house, cinema was more easily able to pursue the path of the feature-length narrative film; having left it, the altered conditions have little by little imposed different priorities, among which is the need to kidnap the public minute by minute and ecstasy by ecstasy. The challenge today is probably to make movies for an audience outside the dark cube, and talents like Wong Kar-Wai, Park Chan-Wook, Nicolas Winding Refn, and Paolo Sorrentino already suggest that a great cinema built upon stylistic intensification (slow motion, obsessive use of music, original framing, elliptical editing) is possible.

Is a "cinema by vocation anthological," as Barthes liked to define Eisenstein's work, awaiting us? Films such as *In the Mood for Love*, *Drive* or *Old Boy* would lead us to believe—or at least hope—so. But they are only annunciations of something that does not yet exist. Perhaps we just need to be patient. In the 1930s an entire generation thought it sufficed to film the major Broadway successes with famous actors; today another generation is content simply to keep in touch with the public. That by now this is a necessary but not sufficient condition; that moving images' Pavlovian nature must be exploited, not borne; that stylistic intensification and the aesthetic of the shark, the baby, and the pin-up girl are at most the preamble of a cinema yet to come—these now somehow begin to seem like foregone conclusions. The shape that directors' experiments will take, however, remains unpredictable. But at least one thing is certain: the battle is being fought in the flow of moving images—without Vitruvius's support and complicity, which meant so much to the last century's films.

6

Desdemona Must Die

I was compromised; the young widow who wept on the screen was not I,
and yet she and I had only one soul.

Jean-Paul Sartre, *The Words*

How could you not cry at Griffith's Broken Blossoms?

Gilles Deleuze

After the long hegemony of semiotics and psychoanalysis, in the last twenty years or so film theory has resurfaced. In some cases, thanks to neuroscience, we have been forced to reconsider everything we thought we knew about how movies work. For example, Noël Carroll and the American Cognitive school have insisted that it is a mistake to describe the director–spectator relationship in terms of linguistic communication (cinema, notwithstanding what we have been told, is not a language, and has no grammar or vocabulary). For this reason, it would be more useful to speak of the director's work as *attention management*: controlling the audience's attention by editing small blocks of frames. The filmmaker chooses in advance what the viewer will see—for how long, from what distance and perspective, in what order—and requires him to concentrate, frame after frame, on the images chosen for him. In other words, the director takes the spectator by the hand, making him respond to visual and audio stimuli according to a predetermined script. There is no escape: unlike theatre, where the eye is free to wander about the scene, a film lets us see only what we are given to look at. And this is precisely why in the 1950s Bazin spotted in the deep focus of Jean Renoir's,

Roberto Rossellini's, and Orson Welles's films the coming of a more democratic cinema, in which anyone could choose what to watch.

Obviously, this is not the place to dwell on how we might reconceive of films as "images to be seen" instead of "texts to be read." Nonetheless, this depiction of the director's work indirectly confirms the arguments in previous chapters on the picture house's role in the aesthetic experience. If Carroll is right (and I think he is), and each film is constructed so as to win the audience's attention and administer it according to the screenplay's needs, all that can be said of cinema in the age of individual media is that the internet, TV, and the DVD do not necessarily produce more distracted spectators, but rather require us to rethink the instruments that solicit their attention. No surprise, given that New Hollywood's visual and narrative style changed in response to the end of the movie house monopoly.

This is where it all starts. Cinema's recent stylistic intensification is the first and most undeniable result of the Vitruvian spectacle's crisis. In particular, the idea that the public's freedom in front of the television has encouraged a precise evolution of films seems a fair reconstruction of what has happened in recent decades. But there is more. If the end of the disciplining of the gaze that has accompanied the diffusion of new technologies had merely impacted the way films are made, we would already be in the presence of an event of the first magnitude in the history of moving images. Yet, as the auditorium does not simply mean greater receptivity, something much more important comes into play. Just as the introduction of the dark cube irreversibly modified the cinematic experience, the new viewing style is changing the nature of the aesthetic pleasure that spectators seek in motion pictures.

This phenomenon depends partly on the show's changing material conditions. It is not even necessary to follow Baudry's psychoanalytic interpretation, with its dubious analogy between film and daydream, or Kracauer's thesis on the film's ability to weaken the consciousness, to realize that, in the movie theatre as much as in the playhouse, induced passivity guides the audience's reaction. Not that it is easy to evaluate the importance of that constraint and its vanishing in contemporary society; for example, what does the spectator's volatility mean, beyond the obligation to multiply stimuli so as not to lose him? No one seems to have really asked this, partly because scholars have failed to analyze the effects of the regime of necessity moviegoers are subject to during a projection. Until we know just what theatre and cinema owe to architecture, it will be difficult to assess the consequences of moving images' liberation from the dark cube.

Fortunately there are exceptions. Among contemporary thinkers, American philosopher Stanley Cavell has probably done the most to focus on the spectator's physical condition, having in fact designed an elaborate dramatic theory entirely built on the onlooker's immobility. His intuitions reach far beyond the tremendously acute reading of Shakespeare's *King Lear* in which he sketches them and are thus particularly useful for explaining how the aesthetic experience of watching movies is transformed once freed from the dark cube's disciplining grip. But one step at a time.

Just as Greenaway would do with the movie house about twenty years later (Cavell's essay is from 1969), Cavell begins by acknowledging the unnaturalness of theatre's social conventions. "[T]he first task of the dramatist," he writes, "is to gather us and then to silence and immobilize us. Or say that it is the poster which has gathered us and the dimming house lights which silence us. Then the first task of the dramatist is to reward this disruption, to show that this very extraordinary behavior, sitting in a crowd in the dark, is very sane."

Cavell uses a seemingly trivial anecdote to explain why theatre and cinema rely so heavily on these rituals: the story of a Southern yokel who, during a production of *Othello*, jumps onto the stage, just in the nick of time, to save Desdemona from the murderous rage of a dangerous black man. But rather than smirking at the simpleton who cannot distinguish theatrical fiction from reality, Cavell proposes, we ought to take him quite seriously. As often happens in philosophy, Cavell's yokel is a figure of excess who helps us avoid commonplaces and understand something that we would otherwise overlook. As a philosophical hypothesis, then, the Southern rustic is the descendent of the *insipiens* who is given proof of God's existence in Anselm's *Proslogion* and of the fool of Hobbes's *Leviathan*. But above all the yokel is an alien, a foreigner who does not respect the codes that others are passively subject to, for the simple reason that he does not understand them: a fellow-traveler to the Persians or the extraterrestrials who in Enlightenment novels visit our world and through their continual amazement teach us to doubt our most ingrained customs and put our faith solely in reason. A natural *maestro* of alienation.

Which arguments, Cavell asks, will convince our Southerner that he is mistaken while we behave correctly, that ours is the only legitimate spirit in the face of Shakespearean drama? The most spontaneous, and common, response in such cases is that it makes no sense to rescue Desdemona, since the actors are "only pretending": no one—evidently—will really hurt her. Yet such a response is useless for understanding theatre's essence, the philosopher warns. To insist on the purely conventional nature of the actions represented on stage is not an explanation, but instead resembles the formulae we use to help children overcome their fears. "They're only pretending," is in fact what we say to encourage others to distance themselves from the drama, to avoid becoming too involved, to not enter into it. To escape from an excessively violent emotion.

Cavell suggests that we follow a completely different path. The country bumpkin must understand that there is no reason to interfere simply because there is nothing—nothing—a spectator can do for Desdemona or Othello. At the theatre, our emotions would compel us to take sides, even to rush the stage to deflect the dagger the instant before the killer delivers his fatal blow, or to warn the unaware characters of the betrayal: and this is as it should be. Theatre exists just for this purpose—to stimulate this kind of elementary reaction. Yet such desire is not enough to bridge the abyss that separates audience and character, condemned to live in two different worlds that lack an adjoining gateway through which we can legitimately hope to pass. The rules of the game prevent it. Pinned to their seats, obliged to observe a chain of violence and injustices for the entire duration of the show without being able to modify the course of the lamentable events, spectators are forced to relive and experience the characters' (always losing) battle to liberate themselves from a painful tragic necessity. Any attempt to escape is in vain. "My immobility, my transfixing, rightly attained," Cavell writes, "is expressed by that sense of awe, always recognized as the sense of tragedy. In another word, what is revealed is my separateness from what is happening to them; that I am I, and here."

Such distance is trying, but not necessarily bad, and it is from this collective paralysis that we must depart. For Cavell, theatre's essence resides in the productive contrast between the feeling of belonging to the same cosmos as the actors, who are always within reach, and the awareness that the shadows lurking about the stage occupy another reality, and that therefore any communion with them is prohibited to us. Their proximity (the three, five, or ten meters separating us from the stage) is only illusory: there is no access from one world to another. We can care about Ophelia or Juliet as much as we wish to, but we will never be able to save them.

And here architecture enters the equation. Because spectators suffer the inability, *above all physical*, to partake in the onstage action, the auditorium and its conventions play a decisive role in the drama's aesthetic experience. Forbidding audience members from rising does not just mean demanding their attention, but also becomes a way to reinforce their empathy for the characters. Here we are not far from that conception of the theatrical building as a great cathartic machine that Renaissance architects developed under Aristotle's influence. We might think that, if spectators did not at least in this way resemble Plato's prisoners, it would be difficult for a show to have such a profound impact on them; the condition of necessity they fall into proves essential to that painful empathy which ends in vicarious "purgation."

Cavell's considerations are perhaps even better suited to cinema than they are to theatre. It matters little that he would later attempt to differentiate the two art forms more precisely, specifying that while drama establishes a spatial barrier between our world and that of the characters, film's barricade is moslty of a temporal nature. In any case, the general conditions, at least with regard to the auditorium, remain essentially unchanged. Here, too, there is asymmetry (we see the characters, but are unseen by them). Here, too, there is forced immobility. Here, too, in the end, due to the radical separation of the two worlds, we are unable to stop the story taking shape before us. But it is also possible that technology widens the gap between the two spaces: to "save" Desdemona at the movies, the country bumpkin would have to get into the control booth and break the projector.

On this specific point it may be useful to extend Cavell's analysis beyond his conclusions. If there is a relationship between the spectator's physical constraint and the tragic chain of events that moves inevitably from *peripeteia* to *peripeteia*, in the picture house the cinematic apparatus's mediation and the absence of live actors reinforce this inexorability. Everything is already written. For the audience, in movies, fate advances at a rhythm of twenty-four frames per second—as implacable, merciless, unstoppable as the mechanism that brings Oedipus to kill his father and lie with his mother, or Orestes to vindicate Agamemnon by killing Aegisthus and Clytemnestra. A veritable Technological Destiny, where the film that plays seems to offer a modern allegory made of the thread of life woven by the Three Fates: Clotho ("the spinner"), Lachesis ("the drawer of lots"), and Atropos ("the inevitable"), whose task it is to sever the spindle fiber in one fell swoop.

As with the artificial nightfall and the strict separation of stage from house, the dark cube turns out to be a more rigorous, and therefore more effective, aesthetic device than its sixteenth-century forebear. Thanks to technology, dramatic necessity reaches its apex; in fact, as Marcel Proust writes of the magic lantern (which is cinema's ancestor) in his *In Search of Lost Time*, "nothing could stop his slow horseback ride." Perhaps for this reason there are few cinematic experiences as distressing as the one where the film spills a blaze of bubbles onto the screen and snaps in two. Suddenly the toy is broken; the tragedy machine falters and the spectator remains momentarily disoriented, as if the incident may have forever compromised his ability to let himself be fooled. So it is not at all strange that directors from Ingmar Bergman (in *Persona*) to Giuseppe Tornatore (in *Cinema Paradiso*) have felt compelled to put this upsetting occurrence on screen in a sort of apotropaic gesture that reminds us of the fragility of the rite.

Here, too, the bond between theatre and cinema is confirmed. The basic mechanism remains the same, but with cinema, as we have seen, the disciplining of the audience's emotion reaches a perfection that makes the dark cube the promised land of make believe—the consummation of the Renaissance architects' aesthetic–pedagogic project. Even the idea, commonly repeated since the 1910s, that cinema represents a *sui generis* form of mesmerism or hypnosis of the masses (thinking, for example, of *The Cabinet of Dr. Caligari* or the *Mabuse* series) is merely the result of this precocious awareness of its unprecedented power over the audience: the power of film, certainly, but also the power of Auditorium–Destiny.

The spectator's position in front of the TV is something else entirely. If cinema is in fact the fullest realization of the Italian playhouse's potential, television takes its inspiration from completely different hypotheses. The audience's freedom radically changes its expectations, as we see in the way we respond to the unexpected interruption of the flow of images. Whereas the film's snapping is a negation, if not an outright profanation, of cinema's very principles, TV news and variety shows consider such glitches an involuntary celebration of their live status, and it is no longer a secret how many of these presumed "accidents" are purposely designed.

This is of course an extreme case. More generally, our ability to choose our viewing conditions (either more or less like theatrical screening) or to not watch—typical possibilities of individual media—means that the viewer is more inclined to accept external interruptions, including commercials. Outside of the dark cube, cutting the emotional tension is simply no longer taboo. As we have seen, in fact, the various post-cinematic viewing styles share not only the objective degradation of the images and sound, but also the disappearance of the shackles that bind spectators.

In the transition from silent to sound films, various American journalists had recourse to a parallel with Caesar's crossing of the Rubicon: *Alea iacta est*, the die is cast. Even in the absence of a symbolic date, such an image—a sign of technology's irreversibility—is well suited to the contemporary situation. As a medium, television seems expressly conceived to reject the knowledge of Renaissance architects and theoreticians and disavow that disciplining of the gaze set in motion by the Italian playhouse, beginning perhaps with the severe admonitions of the Aristoteleans against the *interme\u007fi*—the performances given during the main show's intermissions. As Angelo Ingegneri put it,

> *Interme\u007fi* should not be done, because they are by necessity either comic or tragic. In the latter case, the argument will either be the same or different from the main drama. If the same, the public will have difficulty distinguishing it from the principal story (since the audience mainly comprises ignorant people) and will be confused about the actions represented. If instead the topic of the *interme\u007fo* is different, the spectators, forced to follow multiple stories at the same time, will confuse the plots and be unhappy with both of them. But if the *interme\u007fi* are comic, the problem becomes even more serious. While in fact the dramatist attempts to incline the spectators to commiseration and terror, the players' jokes will distract them and the same thing will happen to them that befalls a sick man who, alternating his medicine with food and drink unsuited to his condition, thwarts his cure [*purga*].

The post-cinematic public is deaf to such arguments. Even closeness to the characters—once strengthened by the physical restraints of collective viewing—has diminished now that we have control over the images we see. We can absent ourselves from the show whenever we like; and even if we remain until the end, in front of the television it will be difficult to feel for the unhappy Othello and Desdemona with the same passion that the auditorium arts require of us. The simple fact of finding ourselves in a condition of non-necessity makes seeing a film on TV completely different. A self-imposed obligation, which can continuously be revoked by the one who faces it, is not a true obligation, as Niccolò Machiavelli (expressing his doubts about stoic attitudes and virtues unsupported by solid external compulsion) repeatedly pointed out around the time that the humanists were working to systematize the modern theatre building. As a matter of fact, all it takes to compromise the total immersion theorized by the inventors of the Italian playhouse is the possibility of detaching ourselves from the chain of events with a touch of the remote.

It could not be any other way. Outside of the theatre, and with an instrument like the remote control, we are much less inclined to develop that empathy which is so essential in triggering catharsis. We will still probably decide to watch the Moor of Venice's story again, and we are likely to be moved by his jealousy once more. Yet something in the mechanism could still get stuck from the moment we cease to share with the shadows on screen the lack of freedom that makes us so similar to them.

Through his argument on the spectator's forced immobility and helplessness, Cavell offers original reflections on theatre's morality that are invaluable for an investigation of moving images in the age of individual media. First, he rejects the notion, presented somewhat bitterly by an entire anti-Aristotelean tradition from Jean-Jacques Rousseau to Brecht to Augusto Boal, that the theatre's physical constraint delivers us to acquiescence and lack of interest in others. On the contrary, for Cavell, reinforcing the sense of impotence deepens the public's participation in the characters' suffering. From this point of view, in fact, the vigilant and even turbulent immobility of Cavell's spectators has nothing to do with the relaxation evoked by the scholars who equate the cinematic experience with sleep or hypnosis; unpleasant as it is, if anything it may prompt us to think of *A Clockwork Orange*'s terrible "Ludovico Technique."

The theatrical or cinematic spectator's stasis, then, is a preamble to action. We would like to intervene, but we cannot. Yet this very discomfort is the theatrical experience's most precious fruit—a sort of vaccine, taken in small doses, with the power to stimulate the antibodies necessary for civic life. Men and women, Cavell explains, are always exposed to the risk of treating others as if they were nothing more than simple appearances: extremely realistic figures we encounter without their interior lives touching us in any real way. We are talking about a very concrete danger here. Philosophical solipsism and the radical skepticism of Descartes—that is, the temptation to think that other living beings are nothing more than projections of our brain or the trickery of an evil genius—according to Cavell are simply the intellectually sophisticated variants of a sentimental torpor that threatens us at any given moment. Every day we hover between passing indifferently by and getting mixed up in the existence of the strangers we share a few seconds with on the sidewalk, in a subway car, or at the counter of a coffee shop. Do I have to do something for that man who asks me for money to eat, or can I tell myself yet again that his problems do not concern me? And that girl who is screaming, fifty feet away from me, in the middle of the park? Do I have to run to her aid even if I am late for an important meeting? The choice to let ourselves be touched—or not—by the stories and the lives that glimmer behind these fleeting apparitions is ours and ours alone.

Here theatre (and cinema) come into play. For Cavell, the principal lesson of drama, and of tragedy in particular, is that the reciprocal recognition we are unable to achieve during a performance or screening—given our inability to intervene in the characters' lives—constitutes the essence of human relationships. Unlike in the theatre, in our daily life we can and must break the asymmetry: let ourselves get involved; leave the dark; allow others to look at us, discover us as individuals, and reveal themselves to us at the same time. Until we take this decisive step, the process of suffering and purification that belongs to theatre (but, again, to cinema as well) will remain incomplete. Refusing to recognize others as human beings and expecting them to do the same would mean reducing them to a source of aesthetic pleasure, as if they were not flesh and blood, but rather characters performing for us on an unreachable stage (or screen). We would be behaving, that is, like Homer's gods, who from the timeless tranquility of Olympus take pleasure in the mortals' strife and misadventures.

Because the two worlds are strictly separated, tragedy exempts us from the obligation to save Desdemona; however—Cavell suggests— we might legitimately think that this happens only so that we are better able to perform this task once we leave the theatre. The physical immobility (the necessity that unites tragic character and spectator, until that last drop of blood is spilt) predisposes us to make the moral choice, precisely because fear and emotion compel us to react, only then to realize that intervention would be useless anyway. This is why tonight Desdemona's life will be cut short even though Othello did not hide his criminal intentions from us:

Put out the light, and then put out the light:
If I quench thee, thou flaming minister,
If I can again thy former light restore,
Should I repent me; but once put out thy light,
Thou cunning'st pattern of excelling nature,
I know not where is the Promethean heat
That can thy light relume. When I have pluck'd thy rose
I cannot give it vital growth again,
It needs must wither.

Since theatre provides our education through forced immobility, the architecture that obligates us to sit still plays a decisive role. If in fact we cannot interrupt the performance, at least we can take away precious lessons from the experience. Our feelings for Desdemona (for whom there is nothing we can do) will act as a stimulus to our actions in the real world, where we are not chained to a spot, in the dark, and we can fight until our choices make a difference.

From theatre, then, comes a paradoxical lesson that would not displease the French existentialists. Instead of being a brake, the audience's voluntary captivity is in the end the most powerful impulse to action. With respect to Aristotelean catharsis, the emotion Cavell speaks of is in fact uniquely capable of liberating the spectator, pushing him to practice in real life the empathy that in the theatre has no outlet. We are paralyzed, but all at once inertia, dread, silence, and immobility (everything Rousseau so detested) become indispensable to the next liberation, when outside the theatre our choices will once again matter.

Until then, opposition will be perfectly useless. For this reason the ancient stoic maxim *fata volentes ducunt, nolentes trahunt* ("The fates lead the willing, the unwilling they drag away") best describes the cinematic and theatrical experience, where Cavell's yokel is the man taken by force and the spectator accustomed to the fiction's rules instead embodies the sage who has learned to profit from his own impotence. And yet all this—as we have seen—represents the past. The absolute freedom spectators enjoy today, in the individual media age, has put an end to the cognitive and psychological process Cavell describes. For this reason, if

he is right, in the shattering of the classical dramatic mechanism we spot
a form of freedom from necessity, but also a net loss. Without immobility, even our desire to run to the rescue of the million Desdemonas who
inhabit our world, moved by the memory of the one we can do nothing
for, seems destined to evaporate. In front of the television, the easiest
response to a really overpowering scene will always be to change the
channel.

The problem is at once aesthetic and moral. For Cavell the paralysis
that renders empathy possible is also the first step toward the acknowl-
edgment of others. But what happens if this coerced immobility
suddenly disappears, not only because I can continually deflect the
chain of events by chatting or reading a newspaper, but because I can
change it at will? To refuse the suffering means to refuse the catharsis.
Following this path, television twice rejects the spectator model characteristic of the auditorium arts—first, because it permits us
instantaneously to avert our gaze when the images are not to our
liking, but more so because it gives us the illusion of not being prisoners: that is, of being able to interfere in the tragic chain of events
without getting involved in the game.

Clotho, Lachesis, and Atropos have never been so far away. If in fact
the yokel corresponds to the man who seeks to escape from his own
destiny (and for this is mistreated), while the public educated in the
pleasures of theatre or cinema represents the sage who lets himself be
guided by the events (and thus manages to benefit), the small screen
simply coincides with the disappearance of Destiny, the Latin *fata*. It
does not make sense, then, to castigate television viewers because at
home they do not watch movies with the same attention they exhibit at
the picture house, as if viewing styles were totally indifferent to technological devices and as if the TV and the remote were not designed
expressly to realize this rapid emancipation from the movie theatre's
codes. Independently of what it transmits, as an aesthetic device the
television set requires that we are released from the realm of necessity—
beginning with our attitude toward the images we see.

The most acute interpreters of the new civilization of moving images
understood this back in the 1980s. "Zapping," wrote Serge Daney,

has always been an invention of the television, it is intrinsic to it and, zapping like madmen, we limit ourselves to generalizing the use of it and to putting the concept into practice. Since the ball entered the viewer's court, he has vindicated his ex-passivity, taking normal television use to its extreme, a normal use that consists of interrupting everything.

The zapper is unaware of, and does not deserve criticism for, having chosen to explore so radically all of the possibilities the device offers, even if his experiments with the remote control will annihilate the model of the spectator characteristic of the auditorium for the last 500 years.

Television, moreover, does not operate on its own. Beginning in the 1980s this *crisis of necessity*—let us call it that—was further privileged by the progressive diffusion of individual image-reproduction systems like the VCR, and, later, the DVD and Blu-ray player. Though, thanks to the video cassette, the small screen became the natural headquarters of the year's best cinema, the possibility of viewing old films at one's pleasure created a turning point in the history of moving images comparable to that of the remote control. Rewinding was for some time the reader's prerogative only; with the exception of operatic encores, nothing similar was available to theatre or cinema attendees. But this impossibility—far from being a lack—instead reinforced the common impression that everything that happened on stage or screen was somehow subjected to a greater necessity. Were not theatre and cinema, and tragedy in particular, the land of the Irreversible? "When I have pluck'd thy rose,/ I cannot give it vital growth again," the Moor of Venice rightly says, condensing into a single line the absurdity of the need, which every dramatic character comes up against, to undo what has already been done.

Unlike theatre, cinema directly incorporated into its technology this notion of existence as an irrevocable chain of events. Once the machines are put into action (the machine of the plot and the machine of the projector), they proceed on their own, with the somber obstinacy of fate. Irrespective of genre, no film was exempt from this universal principle, and it was so until the invention of the spectator–projectionist put an end to audience passivity. When the remote control arrived, for the first time the spectator experienced the pleasure of being free, but it was the video recorder that definitely placed the film completely at her disposal. Partly for this reason, the novel possibility of rewinding makes the videotape and DVD—even more than the remote control—exemplary cases of the ways in which technology influences viewing style, and this in turn transforms the aesthetic experience. By way of the video recorder, along with the option of fast-forwarding and skipping scenes, spectators began to enjoy viewing and re-viewing a sequence, a fragment of a sequence, even a single frame, as desired—potentially ad infinitum.

If the theatrical or cinematic device seems purposely designed to make the audience feel the physical impossibility of escaping the dramatic mechanism, the new image-playback systems reject this irreversibility. With their promise of stopping or inverting the advance of time, they seem to offer a surrogate for the "Promethean heat" with which Othello dreams of bringing his love back to life. But this power is an obstacle to the grief that goes along with every great aesthetic experience. Freed from necessity, we will have to work harder to identify with the characters' troubles, to suffer their and our own impotence. And this because—contrary to what theatre and then cinema for centuries tried to do—the viewing style of the individual media age has no intention of reinforcing identification, but instead makes us attend to the misfortunes of different characters with the same cool distance we feel when we hear stories about people who have nothing to do with us. The remote offers us shelter: it is the shield that makes our indifference possible, but also the instrument of our refusal to suffer with the imaginary beings who live and breathe in the images before us.

All this, of course, relates to models of spectatorship, and is indifferent to the kind of films that are projected or transmitted. It is possible, for example, that on the small screen the vicissitudes of Antoine Doinel or Scarlett O'Hara still sets our hearts aflutter just as in a movie theatre; but this happens to some extent *against* the very essence of television, and only as long as we renounce some of video's possibilities. Empathy may not be automatically impossible, but the post-cinematic viewing style dissuades us from becoming engaged beyond a certain degree.

There is a lot of talk about television's effects on young viewers—a theme that obsesses parents, sociologists, pedagogues, clergy, and columnists of every kind, and has to do only partly with the transformation of the aesthetic experience in the age of individual media. Nonetheless, it is worth dedicating at least a few words to the issue. Those who condemn the small screen's dangers and potential immorality with this term—immorality—for the most part refer to explicit representations of sex and violence on the networks, especially during the day and prime time, when large numbers of minors will more likely gather to watch. In an attempt to stem the phenomenon, each year parents' organizations inform us, with an abundance of data, how such shows will influence adolescent psychological maturation and behavior. Homicides. Pornography. Excesses of every kind. In the face of such a mobilization, not even politicians remain deaf to the alarm. In 1999, for example, a speech by then US President Bill Clinton on the consequences of unsupervised exposure to television programs received much attention from the international media. Because the argument was nothing new, on that occasion what most impressed journalists were the astronomical figures which, supplied by such an authoritative personality, had an air of reliability. Between films, TV movies, and TV series, an eighteen-year-old American would already have seen 200,000 scenes of violence and 40,000 homicides: an average of seven in 350 characters killed every evening in prime time (one in fifty, or 2 percent). Was all this exposure to every kind of barbarism really not going to have some effect on the young minds of television viewers, Clinton asked, or was it time that politicians took serious responsibility for the problem—even at the cost of revisiting some of the most deep-seated convictions about censorship and freedom of expression?

There was not much agreement, and since then discussion of the issue has not stopped—though more recently the internet seems to have become the principal target of similar attacks. It is possible, even probable, that such worries are not entirely unfounded; however, put in these terms, the question betrays a certain coarseness of thought. In equal measure to literature, theatre, and cinema (but certainly with a much greater power of penetration), television would be beneficial or detrimental only by virtue of its content, in the same way as it might be good or bad company. In short, there are those who believe that some additional fade-outs are enough to resolve the problem. But summarizing the question this way automatically makes it ridiculous (and many of the debates are in effect ridiculous), starting with the statistics. One in every fifty characters killed? Undisputed masterpieces of Western literature like Sophocles' *Antigone* or Aeschylus's *Orestia* carry much higher percentages (even if Athenian dramatists were prohibited from allowing the deaths to happen on stage); a quick count shows that Seneca, Shakespeare, and Marlowe offer even less reassuring numbers, while the tragedies of Racine, Corneille, Schiller, and Alfieri have death rates nearer to that of the Greeks. Evidently the problem—if there truly is a problem—lies elsewhere.

Let us be clear on one point. Television is not simply a ubiquitous cine-franchise that lacks the zealous, scowling cashier who checks the youngest spectators' IDs before letting them enter the auditorium—even if this unfortunately seems to be the prevaling notion among those who claim to be so concerned with the small screen's evil effects. The contents of a film broadcast on television may appear to us either harmless or harmful, just as nothing prevents us from discussing directors' stylistic choices in terms of ethics or responsibility. In the same way, it is not hard to imagine good arguments against prime-time showings of art films like Nagisa Oshima's *Realm of the Senses* or Pier Paolo Pasolini's *Salò*, for fear of the influence the images might have on a public including children and adolescents. But, alas, none of this tells us anything about the particularity of the television medium.

Most of TV's critics insist on the dangerous imitative phenomena it could trigger in younger viewers. In the speech cited earlier, for example, Clinton spoke generally of studies that identified the difficulty children have in distinguishing between fantasy and real violence. According to Clinton, and almost everyone who has worked on the problem, this inability to tell reality from fiction results in a dangerous tendency to repeat the actions seen on screen. Here we are not that far away from Cavell's yokel who rushes to Desdemona's aid because he confuses Othello for a real killer—though in this case, the pedagogues' concern seems to be that children can imitate Iago. Consequently, "They're only pretending" is the message that Clinton, too, would like to communicate to American youngsters. But is this really the right argument? Once again, there are many good reasons to think not. Only if we live the fiction to its limits does theatre teach us not to reduce the people around us to shadows and to bet on the humanity of others, defeating the apathy and egoism that threaten to destroy us. The morality of theatre, and of cinema, bases itself on this elementary mechanism. But what happens if suddenly there is less confinement, as in the case of television? At the very least, we have to think that the reciprocal recognition provoked by coerced passivity would be seriously obstructed—with consequences we can easily imagine.

At the beginning of the twenty-first century, film scholars seem prepared to wax nostalgic for everything about the twentieth-century picture palace but its essence as a discipline-driven emotion machine. It is not hard to grasp how the time in which we live—obsessed by the dangers of mass media trusts, and for this reason rather susceptible to the fascination of all that is interactive, from internet chat rooms to radio transmissions in which listeners can call in to speak their mind—is the least apt to appreciate a device whose effectiveness is based on the spectator's complete subjugation. However, precisely because criticism of the mass media has failed to address the specificity of the aesthetic experience, it has on this point completely missed its target. For years authoritative thinkers have castigated television for obstructing political action and discouraging every attempt to make our world a better place. According to Hans Magnus Enzensberger and Zygmunt Bauman, for example, if people in the West do not speak out against capitalism's injustices, the fault lies in our being accustomed to representations of pain that, fueling fatalism, contribute to our citizen–consumer passivity. Behind both of their arguments lies—perhaps unconsciously— Rousseau's utopia of the civic festival, where everyone is called to participate simultaneously as spectator and actor: a utopia imagined in pointed polemic against those performances which, as he wrote in the *Letter to M. D'Alembert*, "close up a small number of people in melancholy fashion in a gloomy cavern" and "keep them fearful and immobile in silence and inaction." The logic of Enzensberger and Bauman's complaint is not all that different. Passivity breeds passivity. Already on a thousand occasions, sociologists have contrasted a mythic forum, where each citizen can speak, to the means of mass communication, where a boundless public is only allowed to listen to what a few privileged people on the other end of the line say. Yet if this reasoning is undoubtedly pertinent with regard to free access to information, its application to aesthetic experiences is much less persuasive. In other words, we need to distinguish television as a vehicle for the diffusion of films from television as transmitter of any kind of moving image. Does the condition of necessity into which the spectator is plunged really mean a refusal to participate or to take sides, indifference to others, apathy, and finally cynicism? To think so would be to misunderstand the paradoxical nature of the experience of theatre and cinema, where true liberation requires our being subjected to the most oppressive necessity—in exactly the same way (as in another paradox) that we take pleasure in our suffering (Aristotle) or rediscover the humanity of others through our confrontation with the shadows on stage (Cavell).

A famous eighteenth-century Italian writer Gian Vincenzo Gravina once defined poetry as "an enchantress but healthy, and a delirium that clears out madness." In our time, unfortunately, people seem less inclined to give art this contradictory status, and tend instead to confuse it with a form of communication identical to all the others. Yet, as we have seen, the immobility–passivity–disengagement nexus that in other epochs nursed suspicion toward theatre (Rousseau), cinema (Kracauer), and television (Enzensberger and Bauman) does not describe the spectator's psychological and aesthetic processes.

If Cavell's premises are true, the entire question of television's morality must be reformulated. Television is not immoral (no medium is), but has ceased to concern itself with the education of its audience, rejecting the traditional link between entertainment and instruction. Without pain, without privation, without necessity, we cannot proceed down the path to reciprocal recognition; but this means that the real danger of the post-cinematic viewing style is not so much the possibility of the audience's excessive involvement as it is the lack of emotional participation. Even the irresponsibility of the children who mistake real life for a game ought to be explained as a result of how easy it is—in the age of individual media—not to take their own actions seriously and not to imagine the consequences of their choices (morality requires the constant exercising of imagination), rather than as the result of their gregarious spirits or tendency to repeat any action they see on the big or small screen.

The conclusions of Enzensberger and Bauman are a bit old-fashioned. Contrary to what we have been told, in front of the television we are *not passive enough* to wish to intervene in the course of events. As the movie house crisis has changed the rules of the game, anyone wishing to think about cinema after the Vitruvian spectator's decline needs first to confront the increasingly rapid erosion of the principles on which the relationship between aesthetic satisfaction and moral education in Western society has stood from at least the Renaissance onward. To tell the truth, few have done so, but there is at least one noteworthy exception. In Daney's diary—a goldmine of preliminary ideas on what was at the time the nascent civilization of individual media—we find a remark with an extraordinary affinity with what I have proposed thus far. The French critic reflects on why all of a sudden in the TV age it seems so difficult to talk about the morality of images, and why Godard's propositions on the tracking shot as a "question of morality" seem simply incomprehensible to the new generations of cineastes (the note dates from 1988, and thus turns out to be truly prophetic with respect to all that happened in the following decades). For about twenty years, directors and critics had found truth in the formula that suddenly, for the newcomers, seemed to have lost all meaning. So, what happened? This change—Daney contends—came about not so much because

we have become immoral as because something about the apparatus has changed . . . First the spectator, because he found himself in a physically infirm state ("trapped viewing," darkness, silence), felt solidarity with the actors of the film and sympathized with them (with their passivity in the face of the Author and the Light: the passivity of the "creatures" in the religious sense of the word).

The argument is developed no further, but even in its brevity confronts
the essential problem discussed above. Freer—this is no play on words—
outside of the dark cube, it is ever more difficult to gain access to the pain
that can free us. It may sound strange to speak of a crisis of empathy,
since we are accustomed to thinking of the contemporary situation in
exactly the opposite way. Yet this, precisely, is the most characteristic
trait of our times. When has there ever been a similar abundance of
stories and fictions? It is difficult to imagine an age of human civilization
at all comparable. Not only are we bombarded with films and TV
movies, but all moving-image production has little by little entered into
the gravitational field of fiction that is colonizing documentaries, light
entertainment, and even news. Big stories and small stories, true stories
and false stories (but recounted in the same way): judging by what is on
TV, Westerners seem to desire nothing but plots to follow—and, as if
that weren't enough, plots that simply seek to gain our emotional
approval and keep us glued to the chair.

Is everything the same, then? Absolutely not. In the meantime we
have changed because our attitude toward these stories has changed.
Since the new technologies have invited us to conduct a more detached
relationship with images, putting the two sides of the screen in contact
has become more difficult. For this reason too, conceivably, we are
submerged in fictions—because only rarely do they touch us for longer
than it takes to watch them. And so we are increasingly less able to evaluate the weight of the decisions we are called upon to make once the
show is over, in real life, when the good of the community will depend
on our yes or no.

As with the decline of the regime of necessity characteristic of the
auditorium arts, the exponential growth of stories works to turn them
into just any entertainment. Television encourages a different attitude
toward the same films we see in the theatre—one we could generically
(without any psychoanalytic connotation) describe as voyeuristic. The
new moving-image devices transform every frame into a picture stolen
through a keyhole, or at least make it so that our conduct resembles that
of a sneaky neighbor too interested in the couple next door. Where once
the tragic mechanism entered into action, now we find simple curiosity

to know how it will end. Will they get married? Will he leave her? And her ex-boyfriend? No matter how intensely we seek answers to questions like these, wanting to know how it all works out requires no great emotional involvement. This is how we respond to a piece of gossip that sparks our interest, not what we feel when we are moved by a drama.

Orson Welles was one of the very few who sensed the individual media's anecdotal and anti-cathartic vocation early on. In a 1958 interview he described television as a "marvelous form," but specified immediately that it was a "narrative" form and not a "dramatic" one: "the ideal means of expression for the storyteller." From the context, it is clear that Welles (who would become a talk-show fixture later in life) was not thinking of how films would transfer to the small screen, but of the thousands of different ways the new medium's peculiarity could be exploited; yet his words ring true in a more general sense as well. To say that television is better suited to telling stories than to representing them dramatically is to highlight the device's specific penchant for seeking a less intense emotional involvement, in deference to the continuous chit-chat that, according to Welles, made it similar to the radio. Better suited, in short, to inform us that a man named Oedipus accidentally killed his father and lay with his mother than to make us recognize ourselves in his misadventures. At its best (or at its worst), television does not expect from us a discomfort much more intense than the one we would experience if, instead of Sophocles' tragedy, we were offered a detailed synopsis of it.

People had always gone to the theatre and the movies for countless reasons having nothing to do with the desire to see the show that happened to be running. For a short period, though—in the golden age of the movie palace—it seemed that the Palladian and Wagnerian ideal of a space entirely consecrated to art was about to be realized, thanks to the marriage between the humanists' project of educating the gaze and the modernist sacralization of the aesthetic experience. The television and the remote control declared the end of this utopia. In our story-saturated epoch, increasingly often we ask movies only to help us pass the time; or in any case this seems to be what the new image-reproduction devices suggest. Recently, even the planetary success of reality TV shows is nothing more than the incarnation of a broader change in aesthetic sensibility ushered in by the progressive reduction of tragic experience to news and gossip.

Without the dark cube's disciplinary force, every barrier has collapsed. This does not mean that we have ceased to participate and to be moved, but that our participation and our emotional investment are *qualitatively* different: a sort of reduced version of the emotional earthquake that—from the rediscovery of the *Poetics* onward—every dramatist aspired to unleash in the audience, to entertain or to instruct.

We live in the age of low-impact catharsis.

7

Low-Impact Catharsis

Alas, the effigy of cinema is no more among us. And if, not unlike certain primitive peoples, we persist in acting as though it lived and breathed, if we fabricate objects that evoke or question it, still what cinema once was can no longer be seen. For most of us it is already dead or in its death throes. For my part, I believe it has long since gasped its last, even if, like a god or any natural phenomenon, it may have taken up hiding to negotiate the conditions of its resurrection.

Raoul Ruiz (1995)

The movie theatre is dead, movies are not.

Marco Ferreri (1996)

Not all intellectuals have expressed the resentful diffidence toward the small screen of figures such as Enzensberger and Bauman. On the contrary, in the 1980s—when philosophers like Gianni Vattimo prophesied the advent of a "transparent society" in which the mass media would deliver man from the "reality principal"—new technologies were often enthusiastically greeted as a potential instrument of liberation. Thus it is no coincidence that in those years the audience's release from the movie theatre's regime of necessity frequently received attention from historians who were inclined to castigate the passage to sound films for imposing a more rigorous and restrictive behavioral code on moviegoers. The primitive cinema's anarchy, as much as television's chaos, offered an anti-model to Hollywood and its desire to discipline spectators using the playhouse's viewing style. It was precisely in this key that zapping and the reduced emotional participation required by the newest post-cinematic devices could be praised—as part of a Brechtian polemic against the Aristotelean tragic mechanism, in the name of a radically different art that would lead spectators to become aware of the artificial nature of the work. Would not television also perhaps provoke a sort of alienation?

Today, such a conception of post-cinematic moving images is somewhat perplexing. In reality, aside from the lack of catharsis, the contemporary spectator's emotional distance has nothing in common with the epic theatre's viewing style. Brecht postulated that a shock technique would prevent his audience from being swept away in a flood of emotions (as presumably happens with Aristotelean drama) and instead awaken their critical faculties, enabling them to understand the power relations lurking beneath an unfathomable destiny. But, in his design, skepticism and the refusal of Aristotelean "purgation" were just the preamble to the true objective: to aim the spectator's psychic and emotional energies *correctly* (that is, in another direction).

In contrast, the individual media's anti-cathartic vocation does not aspire to an active public response; rather, it offers a new kind of aesthetic pleasure: a cold and detached participation, where the moment of recognition is no longer necessary (Brecht, significantly, never theorized anything like the reception in a state of distraction with which Benjamin interpreted his works). For this reason, having rejected the dark cube as catharsis machine, the civilization of moving images seems once again to have realized *in a perverse and caricatured form* the projects of the historical avant-garde. Just as in other contexts the aestheticization of daily life, the rejection of the traditional canons, the refusal of art's earnestness, and the de-historicization of the world have come to pass without having opened the way to a political palingenesis that their advocates somehow took for granted.

In all likelihood, the first victim of the disappearance of the auditorium's condition of necessity is that same Brechtian poetics of resistance against aesthetic passions, for the simple reason that today there is less to resist. The general conditions that made coldness and diffidence valuable therapy against the Vitruvian mechanism's psychogogic power having vanished, the epic theatre's strategies are suddenly outmoded and ineffectual because now there is no longer a rough surface against which they can create friction. In a world full of skeptics that makes it increasingly difficult to live a great aesthetic experience, forgoing empathy—if not in its degraded version—simply means going along with the dominant viewing style. If in the 1970s it seemed that any distancing effect was automatically liberating, today those who think that the small screen's massive use of alienation techniques releases spectators from responsibility are probably right: this diminished empathy is the confirmation that the images shown to us, no matter what they are, have only a relative importance.

The problem is crucial for all those dedicating themselves to creative activity today, and a few of this generation's writers have begun to understand it. In the early 1990s, the late David Foster Wallace described a similar phenomenon in regard to television's self-effacement (a classic form of alienation), demonstrating that it wound up corroding the very possibility for that mimetic parody of pop culture that had been one of the principal strategies of the previous generations' American writers, especially Don DeLillo. Foster Wallace's analysis covered both the content and the aggressively satirical style with which most programs treated television, but his discourse would be better applied to aesthetic devices in general. The comprehensive triumph of this irreverent attitude among the mass media was actually prepared by a radical change in the conditions under which people experience the most important (if only in terms of social impact) of contemporary arts: the art of film. There are, in short, precise reasons that parody has established itself as one of the strongest Hollywood genres only since the 1970s, in a moving-image system already dominated by the small screen.

Naturally there is nothing wrong with enjoying the (much less talented) heirs of Mel Brooks or Monty Python, as long as we do not attribute to them a subversive function that they do not and probably never did have. The same could be said for viewing and listening styles: in a completely different context, the actions of yesterday's anti-conformists have become today's standard. To refuse the hard law of necessity and "purgation," the new spectators simply respond to stimuli as the new devices ask them to; but this is exactly what makes the categories of twentieth-century critical thought, beginning with Benjamin, completely inadequate. Theorists who see a promising sign of resistance to Hollywood in every form of "perverse spectacularity" (out of tune with the rules of conduct traditionally imposed by movie customers) misinterpret the contemporary dislike for a classical cinematic story, with its timing and conventions. It is not the proof of freedom and autonomy of a mature public finally aware enough to contest the codes of reception imposed by the majors, but rather the confrontation between an old and a new hegemonic viewing style, cinematic and post-cinematic respectively.

Nevertheless, if the triumph of video does not necessarily bring with it the gospel of a freer world, we ought not to be tempted by apocalyptic prospects, either. The civilization of individual media is not the promised land that some imagine, but nor is the empire's fertile ground being invaded by barbarians. More modestly, it simply coincides with the western world of the last few decades. There is no escape. In part, we have already seen it: an entirely new, previously unimaginable phase has opened, from the point of view of production, style, and distribution. But this is not true of cinema alone. Given the absolute centrality of moving images in our lives, no art is left untouched by the recent metamorphosis of viewing styles. The end of the auditorium's regime of necessity, the exponential growth of entertainment offerings, the multiplication of stimuli, the prevalence of Pavlovian responses (and hence of the represented over the representation), the impoverishment of empathy and consequently of catharsis—the world in which artists are called upon to produce their works and novelists to write their books is marked by the same factors. Not to realize it would be to relegate ourselves preemptively to a rearguard position.

The transformation of the dominant spectatorship model is establishing itself as the great aesthetic question of our time. With it, in the last thirty years or so, a centuries-long process has been inverted. If in the 1900s hypnosis was so often associated with the cinema experience, this is also because people clearly felt that they were face to face with an aesthetic device capable like no other of vanquishing their resistance.

The theatricalization of cinema's viewing style had put films in the position to do better, and for more people, what theatre had only been able to do for a minority. Suddenly, the object of the Aristotelean architects' pedagogy of the gaze was no longer an aristocratic or bourgeois elite, but (at least potentially) an entire population—women and children included.

Thanks to the dark cube's disciplining power, everyone was now called upon to experience and feel that form of modern drama that was cinema in the same way. The intellectuals who greeted cinema as the promise of an egalitarian society were not therefore completely in the wrong, although they were probably mistaken in highlighting its political (and not aesthetic) implications. As opposed to Umberto Barbaro's suggestion, for example, the fraternity of the auditorium was to be found not so much in the darkness that obscured clothing and physiognomy but in the system of constraints and prohibitions that required everyone— rich and poor, educated and illiterate—to submit to the same imperatives. Necessity had never been so absolute, participation never so intense. The darkness, the silence, the immobility, the separation from the outside world, the size of the images, the impersonality of the fate-machine—all worked to impose total concentration on the spectators, to make them tremble as one with the spectral figures on the big white screen. It was the sixteenth-century architects' dream finally made real.

In a few short decades the situation was once again reversed. Just as the auditorium age had been made possible by the new image-recording and reproduction supports' encounter with an antique idea of educating the gaze, the technological progress that followed ordained its crisis. History had suddenly changed course. While the dark cube had represented a strengthening of the Italian playhouse as an aesthetic device, in the 1970s television and then individual media pointed moving images in the opposite direction, toward that form of light entertainment that still today characterizes the way we look at them (regardless of their content).

The end of discipline? A Foucauldian thinker could object that, rather than disappearing, the picture house's rules have been internalized; since by now everyone respects them on their own, the auditorium has lost its purpose. The hypothesis is interesting and, as we will soon see, not completely mistaken. But I think that Foucault's lesson is less pertinent to the evolution from the Palladian theatre to the home screen, or in any case more useful for illustrating the first part of this process (the education of the gaze in the age of the first movie palaces) than the second (the cheerful anarchy of recent years).

Goodbye Georges Mallet-Stevens, goodbye Frederick Kiesler, goodbye Thomas Lamb, goodbye Giuseppe Lavini. But above all, goodbye Vitruvius. We have already seen how this caesura is generally described in terms of an opposition between attention and distraction, and how instead it would be more appropriate to highlight the different emotional responses sought by the various aesthetic devices. Whereas the movie theatre still aimed for "pity" and "fear" (and thus for a strong sense of empathy), television, portable disc players, and videophones instead give ever-decreasing importance to the moment of "purgation" (to use Aristotle's term) and "recognition" (to use Cavell's).

Thanks to tragedy, impotence in the face of destiny and the desire to oppose it anyway are familiar sentiments in the West; through art they have come to shape individual existence. The vastness of the cosmos— the fragility of goodness—the insignificance of man—the uncertainty of the future—the illusion of being able to escape the past: these are all pieces of a conception of the universe that nineteenth-century melodrama and a certain kind of novel had reclaimed in a secularized key, to bequeath it in its turn to cinema, "the contemporary form that most relayed and supplanted melodrama," as Peter Brooks, the greatest expert on the topic, wrote a few years ago. Perhaps it is no longer this way. The last episode of *Andrei Rublev* or the reconciliation scene of *Journey to Italy* will remain moving no matter which support we use to watch them (even if, in the absence of the right viewing conditions, we might have to work harder and the whole effect may be mangled); and yet the great aesthetic and moral experience of an art that devastates is exactly what television seems to render foreign to spectators today. In cases like those of Tarkovsky or Rossellini we will have, at most, tragedy *despite the device*: something far from impossible, even if since the sixteenth century artists from Palladio to Wagner turned to architecture to amplify the public's aesthetic response, as though the text were incapable of obtaining the desired effect on its own.

The theme of the death of tragedy is not at all new; it has in fact hovered about European culture since at least the beginning of the 1960s. In 1961 the illustrious scholar of comparative literature George Steiner published the book that won him international notoriety, *The Death of Tragedy*, in which he argued that only a conception of life like that of the Greeks—where necessity is blind and justice and reason are helpless against the dark forces that rule the world—rendered tragedy possible, while within a completely rational conception of the cosmos like the Christian or Marxist one there was no room for it (Bertolt Brecht and Paul Claudel would therefore be the last great exponents of an art destined to disappear). The argument was in the air, and if we read, for example, the writings of Friedrich Dürrenmatt from these same years, just before and just after the publication of *The Physicists* (1962), we find similar considerations on the impossibility of tragedy in a world in which technology and statistics had thwarted its moral preconditions. "Tragedy presupposes guilt, despair, moderation, lucidity, vision, a sense of responsibility. In this Punch-and-Judy show of our century, in this backsliding of the white race, there are neither guilty nor responsible individuals anymore. No one could do anything about it and no one wanted to. Indeed, things happen without anyone in particular being responsible for them." Even Pasolini's writings defending the possibility of a "theatre of words" and of modern tragedy, from the years immediately following, and Adorno's "Trying to Understand *Endgame*" (1961), with the contested etymology of Hamm from Hamlet, were in their own way part of the same climate. Nothing new, then, if we ask ourselves about the persistence of one of the distinctive characteristics of Western culture in a society that is changing at an increasingly fast pace. But it is possible that the Marxist and Christian visions of the world, just like technology's intrusiveness or the impossibility of making art after Auschwitz, are only partly responsible for tragedy's struggle to survive in the contemporary world. If an absolute experience like that of the tragic (and in its own way melodrama, as secularized tragedy) becomes ever more exceptional in our time, this might result first of all from the transformation of viewing styles.

Not even suspicion of excess is new. Extreme passions have always been seen as a threat to be regulated, ever since ancient Athens, where legislators decreed that dramatic competitions were to finish with a satyr play, so as to mitigate the emotions of the public and permit them to leave the Pnyx in a lighter mood. The community's attitude toward aesthetic experience was always ambivalent: something precious and very much appreciated, not necessarily in a utilitarian vein for its pedagogic potential, but also something abnormal and frightening—an energy, a power to be invoked only with a certain reverence, for fear of being swallowed up by it. This was especially true for the tragic passions. Entire centuries had difficulty with woeful endings of myth, and in the long history of European drama there has been no shortage of librettists ready to deliver Eurydice from death thanks to a surprise ending or the intervention of a god, as in Monteverdi and Rinuccini's second draft of *Orpheus* or Gluck's *Orpheus and Eurydice*. From the sixteenth century onward, the European debate over tragedy centered on similar questions, according to a tendency already criticized by the first Renaissance theorists of the rebirth of ancient drama. "Tragedies," lamented Ingegneri, for instance, "are melancholy spectacles that eyes seeking amusement are poorly disposed to look on. What is more, some think that they bring misfortune and for this reason do not willingly invest time and money in them."

For the most part the debates had to do with the limits that were not to be transgressed because the great aesthetic experience was thought to be highly necessary in the construction of the individual, but it could be harmful if solicited in an ill-advised manner (something that turned every tragedian into a potential sorcerer's apprentice). Compared to this ambivalence, our epoch has developed a completely new attitude toward excess. On one hand, the popular culture of which cinema is a part draws readily on stylistic elements of the past, recombined in new ways each time, demonstrating a persistent predilection for the melodrama's schematic oppositions and Manichean moral conflicts. Great aesthetic passions are considered a good, and movies—from James Cameron's

Titanic to the Dardenne brothers' *Rosetta*—are constructed precisely to unleash them with the violence of yesteryear. So far, then, nothing new. But at the same time, post-Vitruvian devices encourage a viewing style that could hardly be more distant from the silent gatherings the sixteenth-century Aristotelean architects had created for ancient drama. Whereas the auditorium served to bar all that was not directly relevant to the show, creating a gigantic artificial bubble, individual media take the spectator's incomplete participation for granted, and fill in the dead spaces of daily life rather than inviting him to take part in a ceremony. The fundamental aesthetic contradiction of our time lies wholly in the concomitance of these two opposing drives—in a peculiar schizophrenia between a culture industry that approves the melodrama's codes and a series of aesthetic technologies that invite spectators to make themselves vulnerable only to a certain extent, to behave as docile consumers of à la carte emotions. Exactly as with all of the other goods of contemporary capitalist society.

Naturally, this does not mean that until a few decades ago all specta-tors always watched plays or movies with the same attention and composure, or that from one day to the next individual media brought chaos into the *hortus conclusus* of twentieth-century cinema. On the contrary, as we have seen, the movie theatre has always been a hybrid and extremely permeable space, despite efforts to rigorously discipline the audience's reactions. Pure cinema, like pure art, was always only an aspiration; despite Wagner's exertions, merchants always found their way into the temple. In the Teatro Olimpico in Vicenza or at the Opéra Garnier in Paris, in Delluc's picture palaces or at Kiesler's Film Guild Theatre, order and disorder, attention and inattention, were always part of the spectator's experience. Yet this does not change the fact that the last few years have produced a gradual metamorphoses. Whereas once upon a time the aesthetic device worked to build more disciplined and participatory spectators, today the continuous solicitations and the growth of supply encourage a freedom and an inconstancy that—as Cavell teaches us—thwart the conditions of necessity indispensible to the great theatrical and cinematic experience.

The world in which television took its first steps still tended to

separate rather strictly the aesthetic from the non-aesthetic, just as
clearly distinct moments in a person's day (work hours and leisure
hours) were associated with different places and institutions. Since
then, also due to the TV's presence in everyone's homes, a lot has
changed. Art no longer inhabits a separate space, but is dispersed a
little bit everywhere: in design, in publicity, in the shapes of everyday
objects, in the omnipresent music of public spaces and increasingly
often even of public transport, thanks to the thousands of television
sets placed for advertising purposes in train stations, malls, and
airports, not to mention in taxis, trains, buses, and so on. Such a condition relegates the aesthetic experience to an essentially marginalized
role, to being just a filler: little more than background music in the
drudgery of the daily grind.

The most attentive analysts of contemporary culture speak of a crisis
for the art–myth–ritual nexus. Beauty is everywhere and nowhere.
Despite the attempts of the New York and Paris subways to line their
walls and cars with classic poetry, from Baudelaire to Yeats, only literature seems outside of this process, which makes it in some ways
anomalous in the system of contemporary arts: a minority hypothesis
and—at least potentially—a protest, and thus maybe even more
precious. The crisis, though, takes on a specific pertinence in our case.
Bringing the show directly into homes, the TV had a decisive role in this
process, so much so that it would not be so absurd to suggest that the
crisis of the dark cube as hegemonic viewing style was the motor (or at
least the first big signal) of a much larger metamorphosis. Even if one
negates this cause-and-effect relationship, the condition of diffuse,
diluted aestheticity characterizing our time appears to find in the rise of
individual media and the sidelining of the Italian playhouse model its
most perfect realization.

The cathedral of cinema, like all sanctuaries of modernist art, beginning with the "white cube," increasingly resembles a residual, albeit
prestigious space, destined to lose more ground as the difference between
sensation and aesthetic sensation collapses. In the end, the exclusive
matrimony between cinema and the Italian playhouse only lasted a few
decades. Films, we have seen, have already begun to adapt themselves to

the new situation. That the marriage ended does not mean, however, that it did not leave its indelible mark on the moving images that today migrate to many different supports, often without even passing through the dark cube. Not every freedom is the same freedom, not every constraint is the same constraint. And so, predictably, the auditorium's marginalization did not take us back to the first cinema (as some scholars, with a taste for symmetry, had forecast)—neither in the works nor in the viewing styles. The two-hour narrative film still works fairly well today, and television's predilection for shorter formats has not destroyed the public's craving for complex and therefore rather lengthy stories (at least from this point of view, then, the Foucauldian theory of an internalization of discipline seems to work also for post-Vitruvian spectators).

The real change lies elsewhere. Notwithstanding the continuity of genres and (in part) of style, our approach to moving images turns out to be profoundly different. In the post-cinematic aesthetic experience, the strange pleasure born from communion with the characters' suffering occupies an increasingly circumscribed space in the love for cinema. Identification with the character still happens, and the empathy that keeps us tied to the story remains; but both exist in quieter and more contained forms, as if, along with the auditorium, we have lost an essential element of the cathartic process. For those who knew the world of the past, the relatively detached attitude of the new spectators can be downright incomprehensible. Superficiality and lack of interest in images seem to reign. In particular, the generation that came to cinema after the Second World War, the generation of cinephiliac journals and of cineclubs, experienced this metamorphosis as a betrayal: the end of a civilization, maybe even the end *of* civilization.

I have already briefly mentioned Susan Sontag's essay against films on television: a famous text for its deliberately provocative title, "The Decay of Cinema," and for being published in the *New York Times* not even two months after the cinema's centenary celebrations ended (in February 1996)—as a healthy antidote to the thoughtless wave of optimism put into gear by the festivities. Its fulcrum, we have seen, is the question of the auditorium and the spectator. Everything departs from there: "No amount of mourning will revive the vanished rituals—erotic, ruminative—of the darkened theatre. The reduction of cinema to assaultive images, and the unprincipled manipulation of images (faster and faster cutting) to be more attention-grabbing, have produced a disincarnated, lightweight cinema that does not demand anyone's full attention." A conviction allowing no right of appeal.

However, Sontag's piece does not interest us only for its Barthesian rejection of the possibility of a true cinema without the movie theatre. Built upon the equation in which no more dark cube equals no more love for the film, "The Decay of Cinema" declares the extinction of the impassioned spectator who filled the cine-clubs of the 1950s and '60s: "If cinephilia is dead, then movies are dead . . . no matter how many films, even very good ones, go on being made. If cinema can be resurrected, it will only be through the birth of a new kind of cine-love." Sontag speaks with the perfidy of the jilted lover who refuses to accept the reasons for being left; but in the end it is easier to understand such a rigid position on a personal level than it is on an intellectual one. The autobiographical nature of her thought, which has always been the characteristic trait of her writing—the leaven of her prose and her ideas—is here transformed into a millstone that obstructs reflection.

The grand season of the art film, smoke-filled cineforums, the battles between *Cahiers du cinéma* and *Positif* over the *nouvelle vague* or between *Filmcritica* and *Cinema Nuovo* about neorealism, politics, the amours between the devotees of the same sect . . . We can long for that world, now so far away in time and today so heavily mythologized, but excommunicating the present simply will not help us understand the evolution of contemporary aesthetic sensibility, especially given that anyone familiar with the history of cinema instantly recognizes other farewell ceremonies behind Sontag's anathema. The funeral tone of "The Decay of Cinema" is not all that different, for example, from that of the critics and directors who expressed their nostalgia for the old chaotic venues dethroned by the new bourgeois auditoriums that marked the full theatricalization of the cinematic space. Even then the conflict between two models was underway, even then the metamorphosis of the buildings presaged the move from one spectatorial regime to another: "How I miss them, the cinemas of once upon a time," wrote Robert Desnos in 1927, just before the advent of the talkie, when rigid discipline had substantially gotten the best of the cine-variety and fairground cinema. "Auditoriums everywhere are suffering the same decadence as the movies are," he warned, concluding: "But where are they, the old audiences?" It feels like reading Sontag: the same attention to spaces and spectators, the same refusal to come into contact with the new, the same certainty that the end of one *particular* cinema was destined to coincide *tout court* with the death of the seventh art. Whereas we know that, back then, the best was yet to come.

Prejudicial pessimism is a sterile exercise. The current situation is fortunately quite different from the one of which Sontag spoke. Love for the art of the film, as we might well have predicted, is not at all dead. If anything, recent research shows us a multiform reality and a strong tendency on the part of the audience to migrate from one support to another—movie theatre included. Spectators are at times distracted, but they are also inclined to cultivate their obsessions with a competence and a tenacity rivaling that of movie buffs of the past. This is perhaps the weakest point of Sontag's discourse. It is not true that there is no contemporary cinephilia, exactly as it is not true that love for cinema was extinguished once and for all with the neighborhood theatre and the endless debates after the umpteenth *Battleship Potemkin*. More simply, passion for moving images has taken a new form that—if different from that of Susan Sontag's or Robert Desnos's generations—is not to be liquidated a priori. It is possible for example that video players, as well as the ability to download movies, have stimulated a cinephilia of the fragment and the sequence—a cinephilia without works and without authors—that just a few decades ago was simply unthinkable. But this does not make it any less impassioned or radical, or even less learned, in its enthusiasms and in its repulsions (this is the thesis Thierry Jousse and Antoine de Baecque have been defending for a few years now in the *Cahiers du cinéma*).

These very technological processes render possible a cult of images radically different from that of the past. It is here—between the movies illegally downloaded and the contamination of languages, between video and celluloid—that love for moving pictures survives and maybe even prospers, invisible because it is unclassifiable according to the criteria of traditional cinephilia. We cannot exclude the possibility of a rebound. For example, the diffusion of more advanced domestic reproduction systems—the so-called home theatres, equipped with video projector and stereophonic sound—encourages those who have the means to pursue, comfortably within their own walls, a theatre-quality experience that perforce looks to cinema and its viewing style as a model. The generalized establishment of a low-impact catharsis is by no means at odds with the desire to have, exceptionally, a new, more intense, more involving experience; on the contrary, it is as if the retreat of the auditorium as an aesthetic device could make its absolutism more desirable. The right screen, the right sound, the video disc that respects the original film's format, the dark room: to pretend for just two hours—the time it takes to see *The Searchers* or *The Blue Angel*—to be in a real movie theatre . . .

Even though individual media have imposed a new hegemonic spectatorship model, the post-Vitruvian moving-image system remains immanently polycentric. It is also for this reason that, in a world where videophones coexist peacefully with IMAX and Dolby Surround, we can distinguish viewing styles at most according to the frequency with which we adopt them. In the last forty years, cinema has slid from the *ferialis* end of the pole (that which pertains to everyday life) to the *festivus* end (that which characterizes special occasions): something quite similar to what had happened to theatre due to the growth of movies. But this means that the auditorium's current marginalization results not so much in the exhaustion of a particular type of aesthetic experience as in its repositioning in the broad spectrum of cultural goods. At home (with or without the wonders of the home theatre) or in a public venue, the cinematic viewing style today presents itself as an exception—one more thing we must be disposed to pay for. Something, in short, much like the claiming of a cultural status: the certification of superior taste, a factor of *distinction*. Like the third row full of cinephiles in the 1950s.

It is also for this reason that cinema cannot renounce seeking its way in the open sea of individual media. Different supports, different formats, different devices. It is here that spectators today must be pursued; it is here that a new precarious equilibrium must be found, at least until the next technological earthquake restarts the game. For now it is essential to describe the present, in its constituent schizophrenia between an increasingly "warm" cinema and increasingly "cold" aesthetic devices, emotionally speaking: between fragments of the past and slivers of the future. Has the great dramatic experience become superfluous? Does the future hold for us more and more films that are hijacked by their own spectacular power? Or are we simply unprepared to evaluate the forms of expression developed on the small screen, and do we reject them because we misunderstand them? Certainly the centuries-long relationship between aesthetic experience and moral instruction seems to have entered into crisis, even if this does not mean that the same relationship cannot someday, in an altered context, be renewed just as vibrantly (and there are those who already think about the possibility of "experiencing" through videogame interactivity, but this would clearly be something altogether different).

In the twilight of the Vitruvian spectacle, in the face of the crisis of more certain and consolidated categories, it is not hard to understand why irrevocable excommunications like Sontag's emerge. And yet, refusing to come to terms with the new moving images will not resolve the problem. In the future films will increasingly often have their center of gravity outside of the dark cube: economically, stylistically, and also from the simple but crucial point of view of image-consumption. This is an irreversible phenomenon—founded on the power of numbers and destined to impose itself more every day (also through the contagion of the other arts)—because individual media are like a heresy that has conquered more faithful than the original religion, or a colony that has detached itself from the motherland and finds itself suddenly richer and more powerful: desirous to go it alone and to prove itself, finally ready to take its rightful revenge on yesterday's skeptics. We are just at the beginning. And it is hard to believe that directors of the twenty-first century will come to a halt just because we are reluctant to accompany them on their journey.

Bibliographical Note

This book was written in close dialog with a small number of authors: Walter Benjamin and his contemporary disciples (whose theory of reception in a state of distraction I reject as the key to interpreting the spectator's attitude toward moving pictures), Renaissance architects and their twentieth-century heirs (from whom I derive the notion of the movie theatre as a catharsis machine designed to "construct" a particular audience), Stanley Cavell (who has given me the most convincing description of the tight nexus between immobility, empathy, and moral instruction), Serge Daney (who has posed questions about the disappearance of the traditional relationship between aesthetic experience and the morality of images in the post-cinema epoch), and Susan Sontag (whose pessimism and nostalgia for the good old days impede our understanding of the changes underway, even if in her defense it should be remembered that "The Decay of Cinema" was written toward the end of a life distinguished by unremitting intellectual daring). My attitude toward Noël Carroll and the American Cognitivists is more complex, and might be described as a mix of admiration for the impressive thrust given to the refounding of film aesthetics and disappointment over the refusal to offer any explanation for the auditorium's role in the aesthetic experience.

These authors are of course not the only whose work has proved useful to my research; it would have been difficult for this volume to take on its current shape without the early cinema studies of the last thirty years, or Brian O'Doherty's work about the art gallery, to name just two examples. What follows is therefore a partial (and also highly selective and idiosyncratic) list of the debts, large and small, I accrued while writing the book. But here I would also like to mention a long conversation I had with Marco Ferreri just after his film *Nitrato d'argento* opened— perhaps the very first impetus for me to reflect upon the future of cinema without the movie theatre (the citations in this book come from the interview I published in *Filmcritica* on that occasion).

In this bibliography, references to English versions of the works cited are made whenever possible (likewise, throughout the volume, translations have been taken from existing English-language versions if available). Full bibliographical information is provided the first time a source is mentioned; only abbreviated titles and authors' or editors' names appear in subsequent citations. Finally, as a few years have passed since this book was originally published in Italian (in 2008), I have updated the bibliography to include new essays on related themes. On the subject of "relocation," two recent essays by Francesco Casetti are now especially important: "Cinema Lost and Found: Trajectories of Relocation," in *Screening the Past* 32 (2011) and "Back to the Motherland: The Film Theatre in the Postmedia Age," in *Screen* 52 (2011).

Introduction

Francesco Savio's comments on the effects of video come from the opening pages of *Visione privata* (Rome: Bulzoni, 1972).

In speaking of conservationists' and archivists' superior awareness regarding the precarious nature of cinema, its technologies, and its rituals, I am thinking above all of the visionary analysis proposed by Paolo Cherchi Usai in *The Death of Cinema: History, Cultural Memory, and the Digital Dark Age* (London: British Film Institute, 2001 [1999]). On the marginalization of the movie theatre, see also Angel Quintana's judgement in *Virtuel?* (Paris: Cahiers du cinéma, 2008): "We must recognize that cinema hasn't been at the center of media for a few years now."

Enzo Ungari's self-portrayal comes from "Confessioni di un

mangiatore di film di provincia," the Introduction to *Schermo delle mie brame* (Firenze: Vallecchi, 1978). For a "literary history" of the film spectator in poetry and fiction, see the now classic Gian Piero Brunetta, *Buio in sala* (Venice: Marsilio, 1989).

On the increasingly close relationship between cinema and television at the turn of the millennium, a good starting point is John T. Caldwell, "Welcome to the Viral Future of Cinema (Television)," *Cinema Journal* XLV (2005).

1. The Cave and the Mirror

For the image of the cave, among others, see Edgar Morin, *The Cinema or the Imaginary Man*, transl. Lorraine Mortimer (Minneapolis: University of Minnesota Press, 2005 [1956]); Jean-Louis Baudry, "The Apparatus: Metapsychological Approaches to the Impression of Reality in the Cinema," in Philip Rosen, ed., *Narrative, Apparatus, Ideology*, transl. Jean Andrews and Bertrand Augst (New York: Columbia University Press, 1986 [1975]); Christian Metz, *The Imaginary Signifier: Psychoanalysis and the Cinema*, various translators (Bloomington: Indiana University Press, 1982 [1977]); Vilém Flusser, *Medienkultur* (Frankfurt: Fisher, 1992). For Jacques Derrida, see "Le cinéma et ses fantômes," an interview by Antoine de Baecque and Thierry Jousse, transcribed by Stéphane Delorme in *Cahiers du cinéma* 556 (2001).

Before "The Apparatus," Baudry had developed his theory in "Ideological Effects of the Basic Cinematographic Apparatus," transl. Alan Williams, in Rosen, *Narrative*. The Jacques Lacan text I refer to is "The Mirror Stage as Formative of the Function of the I Revealed in Psychoanalytic Experience" (1949), in *Écrits: A Selection*, transl. Alan Sheridan (New York: Norton, 1977 [1966]). Later, Christian Metz extended Baudry's thesis in *Imaginary Signifier*, while Stephen Heath popularized it in the United States.

Enzo Melandri offered a brilliant philosophical defense of the analogy in *La linea e il circolo: Saggio logico-filosofico sull'analogia* (Macerata: Quodlibet, 2004 [1968]).

For a definitive (let's hope!) confutation of Baudry's and Metz's proposals see the first chapter of Noël Carroll's *Mystifying Movies* (New York: Columbia University Press, 1988). In France, Jean-Louis Schefer's *L'homme ordinaire du cinéma* (Paris: Cahiers du cinéma–Gallimard, 1997 [1980]), and Marc Cerisuelo's "La philosophie et la cinématographie," in Jean-François Mattei, ed., *Encyclopédie philosophique universelle*, vol. IV, (Paris: PUF, 1998) presented cogent arguments against the similarity to Plato's cave. As I have mentioned, the most significant novelty in film aesthetics at the close of the twentieth century—the cognitivism of David Bordwell and Noël Carroll—highlighted the multiple contexts in which movies have been shown throughout time but essentially ignored the movie theatre. The rebuttal of Baudry and Metz is in fact to be found only in the last section, "History and Analysis," of their influential *Post-Theory* (Madison: University of Wisconsin Press, 1996), in Vance Kepley Jr's "Whose Apparatus? Problems of Film Exhibition and History."

Remy de Gourmont's text "Epilogues: Cinematograph" (1907) is translated in Richard Abel, ed., *French Film Theory and Criticism: A History/ Anthology 1907–1939* (Princeton: Princeton University Press, 1988).

Ina Rae Hark's anthology *The Exhibition* (London: Routledge, 2002) summarizes the recent theoretical debate on the spectator. Mariagrazia Fanchi, *Spettatore* (Milan: Il Castoro, 2005), Janet Staiger, *Media Reception Studies* (New York: New York University Press, 2005), and Michele Aaron, *Spectatorship* (London: Wallflower, 2007) also take stock of the situation, but their summaries are for the most part derivative. There are, on the other hand, some important essays on the documentary in Jean-Louis Comolli, *Voir et revoir: l'innocence perdue* (Paris: Verdier, 2004), which take a different approach from the Anglo-American studies dominated by questions of gender.

The key text on the twentieth-century art gallery is Brian O'Doherty's *Inside the White Cube* (Berkeley–LA: University of California Press, 2004 expanded edition [1987]). The contextualist theory of the artwork was formulated by Arthur C. Danto in *The Transfiguration of the Commonplace: A Philosophy of Art* (Cambridge, MA: Harvard University Press, 1981).

Roland Barthes's text on the auditorium, "Leaving the Movie

Theatre," can be found in *The Rustle of Language* transl. Richard Howard (New York: Farrar, Straus, and Giroux, 1986 [1984]). It is worth pointing out that Barthes extensively reutilizes Lacanian categories and Baudry's early works without ever citing them; what is more, his reflections were originally published in Issue 23 (1975) of *Communications*, where Baudry's second essay also appeared.

On the economic histories of the passage from cinema to television in the United States, see at least Douglas Gomery, *Shared Pleasure* (Madison: University of Wisconsin Press, 1992) and Kerry Segrave, *Movies at Home* (Jefferson: McFarland, 1999). John Belton's *Widescreen Cinema* (Cambridge, MA: Harvard University Press, 1992) is an important essay addressing panoramic formats' response to television, also in relation to the public's reaction to new visual stimuli.

I have taken Greenaway's comment from *Fear of "Drowning by Numbers"* (Paris: Dis Voir, 1998).

The Benjamin citations on the difference between the reader and transcriptionist come from "One Way Street" (1928), in Walter Benjamin, *Reflections: Essays, Aphorisms, Autobiographical Writings*, ed. Peter Demetz, transl. Edmund Jephcott (New York: Harcourt Brace Jovanovich, 1979). To clarify: it is important not to confuse my discussion of viewing and listening styles with the reception theory of Hans Robert Jauss and Wolfgang Iser; here I am not concerned with the history of taste or the spectator's horizon of expectation, unless these are particularly shaped by an aesthetic device or series of practices (like reading silently or aloud). The public is not in fact a neutral pole of the aesthetic relation but, just like the work of art, is influenced and manipulated by the (social but also physical) conditions under which the show takes place.

2. Toward the Dark Cube

For Julio Cortázar, *We Love Glenda So Much and A Change of Light*, transl. Gregory Rabassa (New York: Aventura/Vintage, 1984); for Italo Calvino, "Autobiography of a Spector" (1974), in *The Road to San Giovanni*, transl. Tim Parks (London: Penguin, 2009); for Jean Epstein,

"Magnification" (1921), in Abel, *French Film Theory*; for Leonardo Sciascia, "C'era una volta il cinema," in *Fatti diversi di storia letteraria e civile* (Palermo: Sellerio, 1989).

All of the descriptions by Louis Delluc can be found in the massive volume of his articles, *Cinéma et Cie* (Paris: Cinémathèque Française, 1986). Philip Morton Shand's words come from his *Modern Picture-Houses and Theaters* (London: Batsford, 1930)—one of the most illuminating books ever written on movie house architecture.

In recent years empirical studies on the auditorium and audiences have proliferated. A good starting point is the collection of books published between 1996 and 2004 for the British Film Institute by Richard Maltby and Melvyn Stokes. In Italy there are two miscellaneous volumes: Mariagrazia Fanchi and Elena Mosconi, eds., *Spettatori* (Rome–Venice: Scuola Nazionale di Cinema-Marsilio, 2002); Francesco Casetti and Elena Mosconi, eds., *Spettatori italiani* (Rome: Carocci, 2006). Also quite useful is the anthology prepared by Gregory Albert Waller, *Moviegoing in America: A Sourcebook in the History of Film Exhibition* (Oxford: Blackwell, 2002). Giuseppe Lavini's quotation comes from his "Il Cinematografo," in *L'architettura italiana* XIII: 9 (September 1918).

For the distinction between orchestra and balconies, see Nicholas Hiley, "The British Cinema Auditorium," in Karel Dibbits and Bert Hogenkamp, eds., *Film and the First World War* (Amsterdam: University of Amsterdam Press, 1995); and "Fifteen Questions about the Early Film Audience," in Daan Hertogs and Nico de Klerk, eds., *Uncharted Territory: Essays on Early Nonfiction Film* (Amsterdam: Nederlands Filmmuseum, 1997). Perhaps the most important book written on the first spectators is Miriam Hansen's *Babel and Babylon: Spectatorship in American Silent Film* (Cambridge, MA: Harvard University Press, 1991). For this reason it seems even more significant that Hansen neglects architecture's role in the formation of the classic spectator. This lacuna is probably explained by the fact that, for her, theatre means vaudeville and the public's spontaneous reaction, not the disciplined (or at least less undisciplined) auditoriums of later years. Such a perspective completely obscures the Italian playhouse origins of the movie theatre, and all the consequences of this parentage for viewing style.

Among the contributions that completely rewrote the history of the primitive cinema, I should mention at least Tom Gunning's "Cinema of Attractions: Early Film, its Spectator, and the Avant-Garde," *Wide Angle* VIII (1986)—perhaps the most influential of his many essays on the topic; Noël Burch's *Life to Those Shadows* (Berkeley–LA: University of California Press, 1990); and André Gaudreault's two works, *From Plato to Lumière: Narration and Monstration in Literature and Cinema*, transl. Timothy Barnard, (Toronto: University of Toronto Press, 2009 [1988/1999]), and *Film and Attraction: From Kinematography to Cinema*, transl. Timothy Barnard (Chicago: University of Illinois Press, 2011 [2004]). Also important are Richard Abel, *Americanizing the Movies and "Movie-Mad" Audiences, 1910–1914* (Berkeley–LA: University of California Press, 2006); Wanda Strauven, ed., *The Cinema of Attractions Reloaded* (Amsterdam: Amsterdam University Press, 2006), which includes a section on the public; and André Gaudreault, ed., *American Cinema: 1890–1909: Themes and Variations* (New Brunswick: Rutgers, 2009). But there are obviously many other interesting studies as well.

The risk of establishing too strict a divide between primitive and classical cinema was precociously signaled by David Bordwell and Kristin Thompson in "Linearity, Materialism, and the Study of Early American Cinema," *Wide Angle* V (1983).

Siegfried Kracauer's reflections come from "The Mass Ornament," in *Mass Ornament: Weimar Essays*, ed. and transl. Thomas Y. Levin (Cambridge, MA: Harvard University Press, 1995). It is quite likely that Kracauer's essay contains a polemic against Paul Leni, the director of *The Man Who Laughs* and *Waxworks*, who, a few years earlier, had argued that it was necessary to capture spectators with a series of live dances before the projection; he himself had specialized in such entertainment. See "Aufmachung!," in *Das grosse Bilderbuch des Films* (Berlin: Filmcurier, 1926). In those years the attack on pre-film cabaret numbers was not only a German phenomenon, however, as it was being conducted in other European countries and the United States as well.

On Charles Lee and his motto, see Maggie Valentine's monograph, *The Show Starts on the Sidewalk* (New Haven: Yale University Press, 1994). Thomas Lamb's quote comes from Joseph M. Valerio and Daniel

Friedman, *Movie Palaces* (New York: Educational Facilities Laboratories Division, 1982).

3. *Vitruvius's Sons*

Filippo Tommaso Marinetti's manifesto "The Variety Theatre" (1913) can be found in Umbro Appollonio, ed., *Futurist Manifestos*, transl. R. W. Flint, (Boston: MFA, 2001).

For the history of the stage, and in particular the Italian playhouse, the following works were most useful: Georges Banu, *Le rouge et or: une poétique du théâtre à l'italienne* (Paris: Flammarion, 1989); Marvin Carlson, *Places of Performance* (Ithaca: Cornell University Press, 1989); Federico Cruciani, *Lo spazio del teatro* (Rome–Bari: Laterza, 1992); and Anne Surgers, *Scénographies du théâtre occidentale* (Paris: Armand Colin, 2007). Of little interest, despite the promising title, is Iain Mackintosh, *Architecture, Actors and Audience* (London: Routledge, 1993). Until today, the only real (but ephemeral) alternative to the Italian playhouse model for the movies was the Cinerama, where the public was surrounded by moving pictures according to a total projection model that might recall Artaud's Theatre of Cruelty, and which today survives in just a few special auditoriums like the Géode in Paris. When it comes to the third great paradigm of theatrical architecture, the thrust stage that extends into the audience, allowing the performance to be viewed from three sides (as in the Greek theatre, or Elizabethan theatres such as Shakespeare's Globe), perhaps only three-dimensional holograms will one day give us that sort of filmic experience.

The polemic against feature-length films comes from Aniello Costagnola, "Sul panno bianco," *Cinema* 28 (March 10, 1912), and "Il lungo metraggio: un passo indietro," *La vita cinematografica* 1 (January 7, 1914), by an unknown author; both articles can be found in an anthology edited by Lino Micciché, *Tra una film e l'altra* (Venice: Marsilio, 1980). The commentary on the danger of cinema and variety's marriage is quoted from an article entitled "Prime visioni e varietà," signed by A. Li. for the *Osservatore Romano* on January 7, 1937.

Benjamin's "The Work of Art in the Age of Mechanical Reproduction" (1935–36) can be found in *Illuminations*, ed. Hannah Arendt, transl. Harry Zohn (New York: Schocken Books, 1969). Jonathan Crary's *Suspensions of Perception* (Cambridge, MA: MIT, 1999) forces us to rethink Benjamin's theory completely. Crary's thesis is in fact that "if distraction emerges as a problem in the late nineteenth century, it is inseparable from the parallel construction of an attentive observer in various domains"; thus the only means of understanding the perceptive and sensorial changes at the beginning of the twentieth century would be to follow both paths at once. On the ambivalent (both positive and negative) nature of distraction in Benjamin's work, see the excellent essay by Howard Eiland, "Reception in Distraction," in *Walter Benjamin and Art*, ed. Andrew Benjamin (London: Continuum, 2005). The long letter to Adorno dated December 9, 1938 can be found in Theodor W. Adorno and Walter Benjamin, *The Complete Correspondence, 1928–1940*, ed. Henri Lonitz, transl. Nicholas Walker (Oxford: Blackwell, 1999). For Benjamin torn between Adorno and Brecht, we have at our disposal the meticulous study by Bruno Tackels, *L'oeuvre d'art à l'époque de W. Benjamin* (Paris: L'Harmattan, 1999). Giovanni Papini's judgment on the spectator's distraction while watching movies can be read in "La filosofia del cinematografico," *La Stampa*, May 18, 1907: by a few months, it is probably the first essay of film theory ever written.

For the "Institutional Mode of Representation" see Burch, *Life to Those Shadows*. See Stephen Halliwell's *Aristotle's Poetics* (Chicago: University of Chicago Press, 1998 [1986]) for the essentially marginal role that catharsis plays in Aristotelean theory, compared to its centrality in Renaissance debates (even if Halliwell, as a specialist of ancient aesthetics, does not interrogate the reasons for the pre-eminence of the question in sixteenth-century commentaries). On this issue, other than Halliwell's annotated edition of the *Poetics* (Chapel Hill: University of North Carolina Press, 1987), see Pierluigi Donini's edition (Turin: Einaudi, 2008).

Sixteenth-century reflections on drama reveal a marked asymmetry: on one hand we have the *Poetics*' commentators little interested in staging, on the other we have the architects and thespians raised on Aristotle and determined to find a practical application for his precepts in live performance; but it is impossible to speak of two completely separate camps. Regarding Renaissance theories on places of performance, we are fortunate to have several modern editions: Leon Battista Alberti's *De re aedificatoria* (1485), transl. Joseph Rykwert, Neil Leach, and Robert Tavernor as *On the Art of Building in Ten Books* (Cambridge, MA: MIT Press, 1991); Pellegrino Prisciani's *Spectacula* (Modena: Panini, 1992); Sebastiano Serlio's *Second Book on Perspective* (1545) in *Sebastiano Serlio on Architecture: Books I–V of "Tutte le opere d'architettura et prospetiva,"* transl. Vaughan Hart and Peter Hicks (New Haven: Yale University Press, 2005); Giovan Battista Giraldi Cinzio's *Discorsi intorno al comporre dei romanzi, delle commedie e delle tragedie e di altre maniere di poesia* (Messina: Centro Interdipartimentale di Studi Umanistici, 2002 [1554]); Leone de' Sommi, *Quattro dialoghi in materia di rappresentazioni sceniche* (Milan: Il Poliphilo, 1968). It is worth noting that Pellegrino Prisciani and Leone de Sommi's treatises remained only in manuscript form until very recently. Angelo Ingegneri's *Della poesia rappresentativa e del modo di rappresentare le favole sceniche* (1598), on the other hand, has only been reprinted in the classic anthology by Ferruccio Marotti, *Lo spettacolo dall'Umanesimo al Manierismo* (Milan: Feltrinelli, 1974), where it is also possible to read a selection of the works listed above. I cite the testimonies of Marin Sanudo on the performances of Plautus and the *intermezzi* from Daniele Vianello, *L'arte del buffone* (Rome: Bulzoni, 2005). Other analogous anecdotes can be found in Marzia Pieri, *La nascita del teatro moderno in Italia tra XV e XVI secolo* (Turin: Bollati Boringhieri, 1989).

The interpretation of humanism as a lifestyle, here applied to the sixteenth-century theatrical reform, is drawn from Francisco Rico, *El sueño del humanismo: de Erasmo a Petrarca* (Barcelona: Destino, 2003 [1993]).

In a field heavily dominated by photographic volumes, the majority of the studies on movie theatre architecture are owed to American and English scholars, probably because their early research was tied to efforts to rescue from demolition the few surviving movie palaces of the silent film epoch. The most pertinent works I consulted are: Valerio and Friedman, *Movie Palaces*; Dennis Sharp, *The Picture Palace* (New

York–Washington: Preager, 1969); Don Sanders and Susan Sanders, *The American Drive-In Movie Theatre* (St Paul: MBI, 1997); Edwin Heathcote, *Cinema Builders* (London: Wiley Academy, 2001); Ross Melnick and Andreas Fuchs, *Cinema Treasures* (St Paul: MBI, 2004). For England, see especially David Atwell, *Cathedrals of the Movies* (London: Architectural Press, 1980); Richard Gray, *Cinemas in Britain* (London: Lund Humphries, 1996); and the monograph series on distribution chains edited by Allen Eyles. I also call attention to the French studies *Architectures de cinémas* by Francis Lacloche (Paris: Moniteur, 1981), and, in reference to the very first phase in Paris, Jean-Jacques Meusy, *Paris-Palaces ou le temps des cinémas* (Paris: CNRS, 1995). For Italy, see Susanna Caccia, ed., *Luoghi e architetture del cinema in Italia* (Pisa: Ets, 2011). On Germany, there remains much work to be done; studies are still focused on particular geographic locations or especially important theatres—for example, Rolf Grünewald, *Der Titania-Palast* (Berlin: Hnetrick, 1992). Generally speaking, these books treat architectural style rather than the auditorium's function as aesthetic device, but they often point to invaluable primary sources.

Examples of incomprehension at how movies work come from Bela Balázs's *Theory of the Film*, transl. Edith Bone (London: Dennis Dobson, 1952 [1949]). In his "The Spirit of Film" (1930), collected with "Visible Man" (1924) in *Early Film Theory*, transl. Erica Carter (London: Berghahn, 2001), the protagonist of the anecdote was a Russian farm manager. For proof of the fact that Balázs's story was merely a foundational myth designed to show that cinema has a language all its own, read Richard Frost, Arthur Davies, and John Stauffer, "How First-Time Viewers Comprehend Editing Conventions," *Journal of Communications* XXXVIII (1998); the essay certifies that the Pokot tribe in Kenya, viewing a movie for the first time, had no need of guidance in understanding the use of point-of-view shots. It should also be noted that studies with children have proliferated in the last few years, and they confirm that people are naturally predisposed to understand films without particular training.

Fred Hood's text appeared in 1907 in *Der Kinematograph* 11, and was reprinted, in German and Italian, in *Bianco e nero* 556 (2006). More or less at the same time, the Czech critic Václav Tille expressed a differing opinion: "This image is only a clip of a limitless reality, it has to make the spectator forget that he is looking at life through a rectangular opening" ("Kinéma," *Novina*, 1908). Frederick Kiesler's citations come from two different sources: "100 Percent Cinema," *Close Up*, August 1928; and "Building a Cinema Theatre," *New York Evening Post*, February 2, 1929.

The perfect definition of the movie theatre as aesthetic device can be read in a brief text by Walter A. Cutter presented in 1948 to the American Society of Motion Picture Engineers. The goal of the auditorium would be nothing less than the "reduction of distraction":

> It would seem that the patrons should know what underlies the successful showing of a picture: Our measure of how successful is the reduction of distraction, is how completely the individual patron is enabled to concentrate on the picture without distraction by uncontrolled noise, faulty lighting, discomforts of any kind, or fears as to his safety if an emergency should come about.

The paper was published as "Psychology of the Theater," in Helen Stote, ed., *The Motion Picture Theater: Planning, Upkeep* (New York: Society of Motion Pictures Engineers, 1948).

Benjamin's appraisal of Brecht is cited from "What is Epic Theatre?" (1931), in *Understanding Brecht*, transl. Anna Bostock (London: Verso, 1988 [1966]).

The evolution of Kracauer's thought on cinema needs to be studied in all its complexity, but there is no doubt that his fears regarding the potentially totalitarian use of the new means of communication intensified after Hitler's rise to power and after his own exile. It is possible that this led to a simplification of his thinking about the auditorium with respect to his earlier writings. The thesis that the cinema weakens the spectator's defenses can be found in his successful *Theory of Film: The Redemption of Physical Reality* (Oxford: OUP, 1997 [1960]). For a sharp analysis of Kracauer's arguments today, see R. D. Boyd and S. K. Wertz, "Does Film Weaken Spectator Consciousness?" *Journal of Aesthetic Education* XXXVII (2003).

Bazin's comments on the release from the mummy complex are of course taken from "The Ontology of the Photographic Image," in *What is Cinema?* (Berkeley–LA: University of California Press, 1967). Bela Balázs on theatre's liberation through films comes from *Theory*. For the concept of discipline as applied to the act of viewing and to the aesthetic experience, see Crary, *Suspensions*. In the *Journal of Aesthetics and Art Criticism* LIX (2001) Arthur C. Danto, Mark Rollins, Whitney Davis, and Noël Carroll discussed the limits of the historicity of the gaze (in response to Wolflin, Benjamin, and the most extreme culturalists).

Harold Rambush's comments can be found in an interview published in R. W. Sexton and B. F. Betts, eds., *American Theatres of Today* (New York: Architectural Book Publishing Co., 1927); Theodor Komisarjevsky is cited in Sharp, *Picture Palace*.

On the pleasure of illusion (film as *trompe l'oeil*) in the primitive cinema, Tom Gunning's "An Aesthetic of Astonishment," *Art and Text* XXXIV (1989) is especially important.

Richard Sennett dedicates an entire chapter of *The Fall of the Public Man* (New York: Knopf, 1974, rev. edn 1977) to the spectator's transformation throughout the nineteenth century.

4. The Age of Freedom

Robert Mallet-Steven's words come from *Les cinémas: l'art dans le cinéma français* (Paris: Catalogue expo musée Galliera, 1924). In the aforementioned article, Giuseppe Lavini insists on the difficulty of designing a space for the new art:

> The arrangement of the auditorium for obtaining more seats that allow the gazes to converge; being able to empty the theatre and get a new public settled in the brief intervals between one show and another; the possibility of continually refreshing the air of the place, which during the show has to block off all sources of light, without creating rapid temperature changes and violent drafts: these important problems to resolve should give the auditorium shape, proportion, and absolutely new characteristics.

He concludes, "We would like the architects of buildings such as these to refrain from letting architectural dogma of the past win out over these needs."

On this subject it is also worth quoting a passage from an unsigned article in *American Architect* (from September 23, 1914) entitled "The Rapid Evolution of the Modern Theatre Type":

> The economy of cinematograph productions makes it possible to provide seats on the orchestra floor and in the balcony at a price so low that the physical effort of climbing to a second balcony would not compensate for the reduced price of the seat. Thus, in a few short years, has a single mechanical invention occasioned a great change in a type of building which was the development of two thousand years.

On the power of light, Leone de' Sommi had already made a suggestion analogous to Ingegneri's in his *Quattro dialoghi*:

> As you know, it's natural for a man who is immersed in shadows, at a distance, to see something illuminated much better than he would if he too were in the light because his sight concentrates on the object, without distractions; or, according to the Aristoteleans, because the object presents itself to the eye in a more compact manner. It is for this reason that I include very few lights in the auditorium, to render the scene splendid, and I put the necessary lamps on the sides, so as not to obstruct the spectators' view.

Wolfgang Schivelbusch dedicates a chapter of *Disenchanted Night: The Industrialization of Light in the Nineteenth Century*, transl. Angela Davis (Berkeley–LA: University of California Press, 1988 [1983]) to the history of illumination in modern Europe. For theatrical lighting in the eighteenth century, see Anthony D. Barlow, "Lighting Control and Concepts of Theatre Activity," *Educational Theatre Journal* XXV (1973)—which includes very useful theatre diagrams. In the article cited above, Papini speaks of "the auditorium's Wagnerian darkness, which prevents the wandering attentions, those gestures and looks, we see too often in theatres that are too well lit."

For Barthes, "Leaving"; for Susan Sontag, "The Decay of Cinema" (1996), republished as "A Century of Cinema" in *Where the Stress Falls* (New York: Farrar, Straus, and Giroux, 2001). Jean-Louis Comolli writes along the same lines, but without the identification of the movie theatre as an erotic device: "What is an off-screen that doesn't open onto the black abyss or the fears of my imagination, but onto the lamp, the bouquet of flowers, the reassuring knick-knacks of the hearth, of the little inhabited, familiar, inoffensive world?" See "Retrospective du specta-teur" (1998), in *Voir et revoir*. Jean-Paul Sartre's autobiographical testimony can be found in *The Words*, transl. Bernard Frechtman (London: Penguin, 2000 [1964]). Umberto Barbaro's passage comes from "Natura del cinema" (1936) in *Neorealismo e realismo* (Rome: Editori Riuniti, 1976). For Barbaro, a communist activist, the darkness equalized customers' clothing and hence the customers themselves (something that wasn't true at the playhouse), whereas Wagner's reforms were inspired by the similar dream of creating a national (not socialist) community of spectators through the theatre. For a contrary point of view, see Boris Eichenbaum, "Problems of Cine-Stylistics," (1927) in *The Poetics of Cinema*, transl. Richard Taylor (Oxford: RTL Publications, 1982). On the impossibility of interpreting cinema as the revolutionary modern art par excellence, Raymond Williams's arguments are still valid—"Cinema and Socialism," in *Politics of Modernism: Against the New Conformists* (London: Verso, 1989).

Franz Kafka's comment on film derives from Gustav Janouch, *Conversations with Kafka*, transl. Goronwy Rees (London: Penguin, London, 1971 [1953]).

The point of departure for the opposition between "gaze" and "glance" is John Ellis, *Visible Fictions: Cinema, Television, Video* (London: Routledge, 1983, rev. edn 1992), as it is for the supremacy of sounds over image (even if in this case the idea that television's kinship is with the radio and not cinema dates back to the 1950s, when we often find it in interviews with Orson Welles). For television as flow, on the other hand, we must return to Raymond Williams's *Television: Technology and Cultural Form* (London: Routledge, 2003 [1974]). In *Televisuality* (New Brunswick: Rutgers University Press, 1995), John Caldwell—the author of the line about the ironing housewife—has convincingly argued against the notion that TV viewers are necessarily distracted and that television is an undifferentiated flow. This of course does not change the fact that the television works in a completely different way from the movie theatre.

There is little doubt that—consciously or not—the origins of the juxtaposition between attentive "gaze" and distracted "glance" must be sought in Walter Benjamin. The notion that television takes spectators back to the nickelodeon age was first advanced by Noël Burch, in "Narrative/Diegesis-Thresholds, Limits," *Screen* XXIII (1982), and developed in *Life to Those Shadows*. It then reappeared in a positive key in Miriam Hansen, *Babel and Babylon*, and "Early Cinema, Late Cinema," *Screen* XXXIV (1993). To tell the truth, with respect to Benjamin's thesis, which reifies aesthetic responses according to medium and artistic discipline, Hansen went even further, attempting to attribute to every social and ethnic group a specific attitude toward films. This led her to argue, for example, that in the primitive movie halls, women were more inclined to talk during the show than men were. Such a thesis was brilliantly criticized, with numerous counterexamples, by Janet Staiger in "Modes of Reception" (1999), in *Perverse Spectators* (New York: New York University Press, 2000).

However briefly, it is worth noting that Benjamin has also been used very differently in the debates over the new mass media society. According to Jean Baudrillard, in "Le point de vue de Jean Baudrillard," *Cahiers du cinéma* 302 (July–August 1979), and Alexander Kluge, in "Die Macht der Bewusstseinsindustrie und das Schicksal unserer Öffentlichkeit," in Klaus von Bismarck, Günter Gaus, Alexander Kluge, and Ferdinand Sieger, eds., *Industrialisierung des Bewusstseins* (Munich–Zurich: Piper, 1985), the Benjaminian aura was merely weakened by cinema, while the disappearance of the traditional relationship with the work of art happened with the great classical films' migration from the big to the small screen. It's possible that this diagnosis is right and that television, even more than cinema or photography, constitutes the decisive watershed in the history of aesthetics; however, we should begin to be suspicious of a reasoning that speaks about the decline of the aura as if it were the decay of a radioactive isotope and that simply removes the rod each time (how long before the same concepts will be applied to the internet?). The exact same defects can be found in Zygmunt Bauman's writings, however fascinating. Francesco Benigno's "Identità come problema," *Meridiana* 55 (2006) was very useful to me in developing my argument.

Hugo Münsterberg's 1916 book was discovered only several decades later, and first republished in 1970 as *The Film: A Psychological Study* (Mineola: Dover, 2004).

I get the division of television history in three phases (scarcity, availability, plenty) from John Ellis, *Seeing Things* (London: I.B.Tauris, 2000).

According to Miriam Hansen, all of post-classical cinema would spontaneously reconnect to the pre-classical cinema, especially in the spectators' behavior—a point of view further developed by Timothy Corrigan in *A Cinema Without Walls* (New Brunswick: Rutgers University Press, 1991). In my interpretation, conversely, the post-auditorium does not in any way repeat the pre-auditorium, but is instead a specific condition whose absolute originality must be insisted upon.

5. The Aesthetic of the Shark

For the nexus of psychology and advertising, of course, the reference is to Vance Packard, *The Hidden Persuaders* (New York: Ig Publishing, 2007 [1957]). On the eyes' reaction to images, Stephen Prince, "The Discourse of Pictures," *Film Quarterly* XLVII (1993), and "Psychoanalytic Film Theory and the Problem of the Missing Spectator," in Bordwell and Carroll, *Post-Theory*.

Serge Daney's reflections on the basic desire to see images can be found in the final section of *Postcards from the Cinema*, transl. Paul Douglas Grant (Oxford: Berghahn, 2002 [1994]). Daney's response to the question, "When is cinema art?" might sound something like this: "The only possible film history is one about that small part of cinema that recounted and theorized itself via film journals, for the simple fact that at a certain moment the process of approaching the real became more interesting than the thing figured, reproduced, or represented" (translation revised). George Méliès's comments may be read in "Cinematographic Views" (1907), transl. in Abel, *French Film Theory*.

Antonio Gramsci's observations can be found in *Selections from Cultural Writings*, eds. David Forgacs and Geoffrey Nowell-Smith (Cambridge, MA: Harvard University Press, 1985).

The line about directors of the 1930s and '40s belongs to François Truffaut, "Lubitsch was a Prince" (1968), in *The Films in My Life* (Cambridge: Da Capo, 1994 [1978]). I take Truffaut's list from the *Cahiers du cinéma* special issue, "L'amour au cinéma," from December 1954. In Italy the leading figure of this type of "drive" criticism was probably Giovanni Turroni of *Filmcritica*; his most important writings are collected in four volumes as *Americana* (Rome: Bulzoni, 1978–88). The US equivalent to Turroni and to the *Cahiers* critics (though with a reduced tendency to eroticize the spectator's gaze) was probably Andrew Sarris. Antoine de Baecque dedicates the entire eighth chapter of his monograph *La cinéphilie: Invention d'un regard, histoire d'une culture, 1999–1968* (Paris: Fayard, 2003) to the eroticism of cinephiliac passion. The constituently pornographic essence of images was theorized by, among others, Fredric Jameson in *Signatures of the Visible* (London: Routledge, 1992). In art history, the viewer's reaction to the content of paintings and statues (often in their erotic implications) was brought into the center of the scholarly debate by the now classic David Freedberg, *The Power of Images: Studies in the History and Theory of Response* (Chicago: University of Chicago Press, 1989).

On cinema in the twentieth century's system of the arts, and its ability to mediate between opposites without losing contact with its spectator, see the acute observations by Francesco Casetti in *Eye of the Century: Film, Experience, Modernity* (2005), rev. edn transl. Francesco Casetti (New York: Columbia University Press, 2008). Naturally, it is not necessary to use pleasing images to capture the public's attention: often the very opposite is true, and some years ago Hal Foster in fact argued that disgust would become the key category of contemporary aesthetics

(*The Return of the Real: The Avant-Garde at the End of the Century* (Cambridge, MA: MIT, 1996). A concise history of aesthetic disgust can be found in the first essay in Mario Perniola, *Disgusti* (Genoa: Costa & Nolan, 1998).

I have described the transformation of New Hollywood's cinematic style with the help of David Bordwell, "Intensified Continuity," *Film Quarterly* LV (2002)—for items 1–4; Stephen Prince, "The Emergence of Film Artifact," *Film Quarterly* LVII (2004)—for item 5; and Fred Pfeil, "From Pillar to Postmodernism," in Jon Lewis, ed., *The New American Cinema* (Durham: Duke University Press, 1998)—for item 6. On James Stewart's and Cary Grant's acting styles, I have followed Luc Moullet, *Politiques des acteurs* (Paris: Cahiers du cinéma, 1993). For a complete profile of the new American cinema with many interesting considerations on television's influence, good starting places are Geoff King, *New Hollywood Cinema: An Introduction* (London: I.B.Tauris, 2002), and *American Independent Cinema* (London: I.B.Tauris, 2005). On the evolution of music videos, see the essay by the very well-informed Jean-Marc Lalanne, "Vingt ans de cinéma et de clips," *Cahiers du cinéma*, April 2000 (special issue: "Les frontières du cinéma").

Dominique Païni stressed the importance of the passage from VHS to DVD with writings on the discrete and non-linear use of film in *Le temps exposé* (Paris: Cahiers du cinéma, 2002).

In general, on the ways in which the "virtual" is changing contemporary cinema and forces us to rethink the questions of twentieth-century aesthetics, see David N. Rodowick, *The Virtual Life of Film* (Cambridge, MA: Harvard University Press, 2007).

The Jean Epstein quote comes from "Magnification." His idea regarding the increasing stimulation produced by modernity's arts needs to be compared to Noël Carroll's hypothesis, based on the most current neurophysiological studies, that we can consider zapping as a sort of homemade editing the spectator does to combat boredom—"Film, Attention, and Communication" (1996), in his *Engaging the Moving Image* (New Haven: Yale University Press, 2003).

Anton Giulio Bragaglia wrote on the stagecoach in the airplane epoch in "La scenotecnica" (*Filodrammatica*, special issue, October 1935). For

Gilles Deleuze, see *Cinema 2: The Time-Image* (1985), transl. Hugh Tomlinson and Robert Galeta (Minneapolis: University of Minnesota Press, 1989).

It is interesting that, a decade or so before shooting *Cat People*, Paul Schrader had theorized the exactly opposite type of film, based on subtraction rather than multiplication of visual effects, as can be seen in his *Transcendental Style in Film: Ozu, Bresson, Dreyer* (Cambridge: Da Capo Press, 1998 [1972]).

The concept of *caméra-stylo* was coined by Alexandre Astruc in "Naissance d'une nouvelle avant-garde," *L'écran français*, March 30, 1948.

Roland Barthes's judgment on Eisenstein can be found in "Diderot, Brecht, Eisenstein" (1973), in his *Responsibility of Forms* (1982), transl. Richard Howard (New York: Farrar, Straus, and Giroux, 1985).

6. Desdemona Must Die

For the art of cinema as "attention management," at the very least, "Film, Attention, and Communication" and the fifth chapter of Noël Carroll, *The Philosophy of Moving Images* (Oxford: Blackwell, 2008), should be consulted. Regarding Bazin's polemic against editing's power to manipulate, I am mainly thinking of "On *Why We Fight*" (1946), in Bert Cardullo, ed., *Bazin at Work: Major Essays and Reviews from the Forties and Fifties*, transl. Alain Piette and Bert Cardullo (London: Routledge, 1997).

Recently the topic of emotions in movies has rightly won much attention in film studies. See in particular the collection *Passionate Views*, eds. Carl Plantinga and Greg M. Smith (Baltimore: Johns Hopkins University Press, 1999).

Traditionally the movie spectator's immobility has been linked to the notion of cinematic viewing as a para-hypnotic state. At the end of the 1950s, for example, Edgar Morin used this idea to reinforce the analogy with sleep, and above all to contrast theatre with cinema based on the role played by darkness during the projection: "The spectator in the 'dark room' is, on the contrary, a passive subject in a pure state. He can do nothing, has nothing to give, even his applause. Patient, he endures.

Enthralled, be submits. Everything happens a long way away, out of his reach" (*The Cinema*). Even before Morin, emphasizing the difference between the auditorium arts served to defend the claim about the film's hypnotic power (and its novelty, compared to theatre). See for example Jean Deprun, "Le cinéma et l'identification," *Revue internationale de filmologie* I (1947), probably one of Morin's sources: "Circular, the theatrical auditorium put everyone right under everyone else's nose. Here my eyes fearlessly follow a path that others respect. The night that welcomes me won't fail me: a safe guardian, it will hide me until the very end." It is unnecessary to remind the reader that this book instead seeks to demonstrate the fundamental solidarity of the auditorium arts.

Stanley Cavell's "The Avoidance of Love: A Reading of *King Lear*" (1969) is a chapter in his *Disowning Knowledge in Six Plays of Shakespeare* (Cambridge: CUP, 1987), and ought to be read alongside his *The Claim of Reason: Wittgenstein, Skepticism, Morality and Tragedy* (Oxford: OUP, 1999 [1979]). His theory of recognition was recently taken up, in relation to the existentialist tradition and Georg Lukács's work, by Axel Honneth in *Reification: A New Look at an Old Idea* (New York: OUP, 2008 [2005]). Incidentally, Cavell's spectatorship model seems essentially built upon contemporary variations of the Italian playhouse, but is not incompatible with the Elizabethan theatre, where the spectators on the ground floor (in fact referred to as "groundlings") remained standing for the entire show while those in the galleries above could sit. Cavell's distinction between cinema and theatre comes instead from his *The World Viewed* (Cambridge, MA: Harvard University Press, 1979 enlarged edition [1971]). It is not insignificant that in this book, speaking about the cinematic spectator, even Cavell could not resist using the traditional comparison with the Platonic cave: another indication of the difficulty in renouncing such a successful simile. It is interesting to note that in the early twentieth century a German philosopher, Waldemar Conrad, had anticipated some of Cavell's questions. "Can we sit coolly by with our hands in our lap when we see Othello kill Desdemona?" he asks. His response, analogous to Cavell's, is that if we do not stop the murder it is only because we know there is no way to change the scene that is presented to us: "We act as if it had nothing to do with people whose words and actions we can influence but with a single moving picture, a talking image, but always only an image, of a biophonic theatre" ("Die wissenschaftliche und die ästhetische Geisteshaltung und die Rolle der Fiktion und Illusion in derselben," *Zeitschrift für Philosophie und philosophische Kritik*, 1915). For a philosophical history of empathy, see Andrea Pinotti, *Empatia* (Rome-Bari: Laterza, 2011).

Niccolò Machiavelli repeatedly expressed his lack of faith in any form of virtue that was not bolstered by an exterior constraint; here it is enough to recall Chapter XXIII of *The Prince* ("men always turn out badly for you unless some necessity make them good") and chapter LVIII of his first book of *The Discourses on Livy* ("all men equally err when they can do so without regard to consequences").

Noël Carroll intelligently defended the television against accusations of being an intrinsically "immoral" medium in "Is the Medium a (Moral) Message?" (1998), in *Engaging the Moving Image*. My reasoning on the non-moral nature of the device, in that it does not favour the cathartic process, is founded on completely different considerations. As the topic of these pages is the influence of the individual media's spectatorship model on contemporary aesthetic experience, my analysis leaves out everything that does not engage this question. On the representation of pain in TV news, in any case, see Luc Boltanski's excellent study, *Distant Suffering: Morality, Media and Politics* (Cambridge: CUP, 1999 [1993]).

Serge Daney's endorsement of zapping, "The Zapper's Salary" (1987), can be read in Jacques Kermabon, Kumar Shahani, eds., *Cinema and Television: Fifty Years of Reflection in France* (New Delhi: Orient Longman, 1991).

Information on Bill Clinton's speech and the data on television violence come from Karl Popper, *The Lesson of the Century* (London: Routledge, 2002 [1997]). Of course the literature on the topic is vast. Scientists are not in agreement on the effects video has on spectators. A few years ago, Barrie Gunter catalogued scholars' hypothesis on the potential psychological consequences generated by violent images into five large families: 1) catharsis; 2) excitement; 3) loss of inhibitions; 4) imitation; 5) desensitization. His essay, "The Question of Media Violence," is collected in Jennings Bryant and Dolf Zillmann, eds.,

Media Effects (Erlbaum: Hillsdale, 1994). It may be useful to highlight that according to some of the interpretations of catharsis proposed by Renaissance theorists (such as those of Robortello, Minturno, and Castelvetro), the scope of "purgation" would be to fortify people, rendering them less susceptible to pity and fear through the repeated vision of fictitious misfortune (as in the fifth point of Gunter's survey).

For Zygmunt Bauman's view, see *Society Under Siege* (Oxford: Blackwell, 2003 [2002]). In "Absolute Emptiness: The Null-Medium, or Why All Complaints about Television are Irrelevant" (1988), transl. William Wheeler (Barcelona: Museu d'art contemporani de Barcelona, 2010–11), Hans Magnus Enzensberger sees the television spectator's activity, including zapping, as the only possible response to the conditions imposed by the small screen: "The viewer makes no bones about having in front of him not a means of communication, but a means of denial of communication, and he is not to be shaken in this belief. In his eyes, precisely the thing he is accused of is what constitutes the charm of the null-medium."

Jean-Jacques Rousseau's comments against theatre come from his "Letter to M. D'Alambert on the Theatre" (1758), to be found in *Politics and the Arts*, transl. Allan Bloom (Ithaca: Cornell University Press, 1960). More recently, in the ninth chapter of *Televisuality*, dedicated to the "Televisual Audience," Caldwell demonstrated how the television industry has learned to work the rhetoric of the spectator's active participation to its own advantage. Jacques Rancière's attempt to avoid the Aristotle–Brecht opposition offers little resolution: "We have not to turn spectators into actors. We have to acknowledge that any spectator already is an actor of his own story and that the actor also is the spectator of the same kind of story"—"The Emancipated Spectator" (2007) in the collection of the same name (London: Verso, 2009).

Gian Vincenzo Gravina's definition is taken from the seventh chapter of the first book of *Della ragione poetica* (1708), in his *Opere italiane* (Cosenza: Brenner, 1992).

The passage from Serge Daney's diary on the morality of the image in contemporary film comes from *L'exercise a été profitable, Monsieur* (Paris: POL, 1993). According to Daney, it is the audience who projects its own paralysis onto the characters, while for Cavell the psychological process should be described as an identification driven by shared confinement; the result is practically the same, though, since in both cases Vitruvian architecture is recognized as having the power to reinforce our sympathy for the protagonist.

Godard first expressed the famous motto stating that "Tracking shots are a question of morality" at a *Cahiers du cinéma* round table on Alain Resnais's *Hiroshima, mon amour* (1959).

Orson Welles's line comes from a long interview with André Bazin and Charles Bitsch originally published in *Cahiers du cinéma* 84 (June 1958), and can be found in Mark W. Estrin, ed., *Orson Welles: Interviews*, (Jackson: University of Mississippi Press, 2002).

7. Low-Impact Catharsis

Gianni Vattimo's predictions come from *The Transparent Society*, transl. David Webb (Baltimore: Johns Hopkins University Press, 1992 [1989]).

On "ironic self-reference" and detachment in contemporary television, the most intelligent pages written are David Foster Wallace, "E Unibus Pluram: Television and US Fiction" (1993), in his *A Supposedly Fun Thing I'll Never Do Again* (New York: Little, Brown & Co., 1997).

The recent abuses of Benjamin's thought by scholars of mass media include the trend of interpreting the figure of the zapping telespectator through that of the *flâneur*. On this tendency, see at least Anne Friedberg, *Window Shopping* (Berkeley–LA, University of California Press, 1993), as well as the second chapter of Beatriz Sarlo, *Scenes from Postmodern Life*, transl. Jon Beasley-Murray (Minneapolis: University of Minnesota Press, 2001 [1994]) and "Post-Benjaminian" (2000), in Hans Ulrich Gumbrecht and Michael Marrinan, eds., *Mapping Benjamin* (Palo Alto: Stanford University Press, 2003). Substantially, for Sarlo, in speaking of "reception in a state of distraction," Benjamin did not understand cinema and instead prophesied television. In general, regarding the failure of Benjamin's prophecies, Gumbrecht and Marrinan's *Mapping Benjamin* is very important.

Peter Brooks's claim about cinema's indebtedness to the melodrama comes from the opening pages of *The Melodramatic Imagination* (New Haven: Yale University Press, 1995 [1976]). On the conditions of tragedy in today's world the references go to, respectively, George Steiner, *The Death of Tragedy* (New Haven: Yale University Press, 1996 [1961]); Friedrich Dürrenmatt, "Problems of the Theatre" (1966), in *Plays and Essays*, transl. Volkmar Sander (New York: Continuum, 1982); and Theodor W. Adorno, "Trying to Understand *Endgame*" (1961), in *Notes to Literature*, transl. Shierry Weber Nicholson (New York: Columbia University Press, 1991). Pier Paolo Pasolini's considerations on modern tragedy are published with *Orgia* (written in 1965 and staged in 1968), in *Teatro* (Milan: Mondadori, 2001).

For satyr plays and the controlling of emotions, see various writings by Luigi Enrico Rossi (significant even beyond the confines of classical philology): "Il dramma satiresco attico," *Dialoghi di Archeologia* VI (1972); and "Il dramma satiresco," *Dioniso: Rivista di studi sul teatro antico* LXI (1991).

The Robert Desnos citation comes from "Salles de cinéma" (1927), in *Les rayons et les ombres* (Paris: Gallimard, 1992).

Thierry Jousse has written acutely on the advent of a new cinephilia without the movie theatre in "Les dandys du câble" (1996), in *Pendant les travaux le cinéma reste ouvert* (Paris: Cahiers du cinéma, 2003), as has Antoine de Baecque in "La nouvelle bobine du cinéphile" (2006), in *Feu sur le quartier géneral! Le cinéma traversé: textes, entretiens, récits* (Paris: Cahiers du cinéma, 2008). But for a more complete analysis of the evolution of domestic viewing in the home theatre age, the key texts are those of Barbara Klinger in *Beyond the Multiplex* (Berkeley–LA, University of California Press, 2006). See also the essays collected by Scott Balcerzak and Jason Sperb in *Cinephilia in the Age of Digital Reproduction: Film, Pleasure and Digital Culture* (London: Wallflower, 2009). On the concept of distinction, of course, the key reference is Pierre Bourdieu, *Distinction: A Social Critique of the Judgement of Taste*, transl. Richard Nice (Cambridge, MA: Harvard University Press, 1984 [1979]).

Index

Index does not include authors or works named in the bibliographic note.